Start of the race "Anything on Wheels"
New York, lower east side, August 6th 1952
(AP Photo/Carl Nesensohn/SIPA)

ON A DAY
WITH

A CHRONIC
SKATE
1779-200

Raphaël Zarka

NO WAVES

UNE HISTOIRE CULTURELLE DU SKATEBOARDING

Éditions B42
Paris

FOLLOWED BY

THE FORBID-
DEN
CON-
JUNCTION

AND

THE QUESTION IS WHICH IS TO BE THE MASTER

© Éditions B42 & Raphaël Zarka 2011.

The author would like to thank: Cécilia Bécanovic, Mathieu Abonnenc, Maxime Thieffine, Guillaume Constantin, Alexandre Dimos, Élie During, Alexis Papadopoulos, Julien Prévieux, Claude Queyrel and Didier Semin for their support and their advices.

The author also wish to thank: Bertrand Trichet, Carhartt, Bischoff/Weiss gallery, Chris Sharp, and Sam Griffin without whom this english edition of that book would not have been possible.

ISBN 978-2-917855-19-5
Dépôt légal, janvier 2011.
B42–19

Éditions B42   80, rue du Faubourg Saint-Denis 75010 Paris – France   info@editions-b42.com
www.editions-b42.com

Graphic design: deValence
Translated from the French by Chris Sharp
Proofreading: Louise Stein

9

**A
CHRONICLE
OF SKATEBOARDING
1779–2005**

89

**A
CHRONICLE
OF SKATEBOARDING
2005–2009**

109

POSTFACE

111

**THE
FORBIDDEN
CONJUNCTION**

135

**THE QUESTION
IS WHICH
IS TO BE MASTER**

141

**INDEX OF
A CHRONICLE
OF SKATEBOARDING
1779–2009**

A CHRONICLE OF SKATEBOARDING 1779–2005

1779
Resolution and Discovery drop anchor in Karakakooa Bay of the Big Island of Hawaii. Captain James Cook and his lieutenant James King are the first to describe the customs of Hawaiians, one being *he'e nalu*, which consists of standing on a long board of wood and gliding (*he'e*) on a wave (*nalu*). *He'e nalu* is a mixed gender and hierarchical activity. The longest planks, known as the *olo*, which are roughly 7 meters long (22 feet) and weigh up to 70 kg (154 lbs), are reserved for chiefs. The tribal people use smaller boards, between 2 and 4 meters long (6.5 and 13 feet), which are known as *alaia*.

1819
In Europe, ice-skating is in fashion. After a number of attempts to transpose this pastime to new surfaces, Mr. Petibled patents the invention of roller skates. The wood skate is affixed to the bottom of a boot and has between two and four wheels (made of brass, wood, and sometimes even ivory) lined up along a single row: a design rediscovered in 1979 by a pair of hockey players, the Olson brothers, before founding Rollerblade Inc. in 1983.

1820

Coming from New England, the first Calvinist missionaries arrive in Hawaii. They have doubts about the humanity of the natives and perceive them as barbarians. *He'e nalu*, which men and women practice naked, is frowned upon. With the arrival of colonists, Hawaiian society becomes very unstable. A number of customs and beliefs are lost and although not officially forbidden by the Calvinists, the pastime of *he'e nalu* is marginalized.

1823

In London, Robert John Tyers patents the *Volito*, a roller skate with a single row of five aligned wheels akin to Petibled's. These early models of roller skates do not yet allow one to make turns.

1840

In Germany, on the outskirts of Berlin, the waitresses at the tavern Corse Halle use roller skates known as "dry land skates" to get around.

1850

Contrary to the Calvinist missionaries, the Reverend T. Cheever, an Englishman, studies local customs and takes an interest in *he'e nalu*. He is the first to use the terms "surf-player" and "surf-rider".

1863

In Massachusetts, James Plimpton conceives the first roller skate with two rows of aligned wheels. Very stable, this model allows one to turn and even go backwards.

1907

The first surf demonstration is organized at Santa Monica beach in Los Angeles. The Hawaiian George Freeth impresses the crowd. An article by Jack London, entitled "Riding the South Surf" published that same year in the October issue of Woman's Home Companion, attracts the attention of Americans. London recounts his discovery of surfing and his meeting with George Freeth during a voyage to Waikiki (Hawaii). The article would go on to be published numerous times with different titles: "The Joy of the Surf Rider," "Surfing at Waikiki," "A Royal Sport," "Psychology of the Surf Board," "Learning to Ride the Surf Board," and "Taming Monsters"; it also constituted one of the chapters of the book The Cruise of the Snark.

1932

The surfboards made by George Freeth are still made out of solid wood. Hoping to make them lighter, Meyers Butte experiments with combinations of sequoia, balsa and pine, which he bonds together with a waterproof glue of his own invention. In order to visually represent the balance and the forces used in surfing, Meyers Butte elects to use a symbol of Indo-European origin, the Swastika, and starts his own company, The Swastika Surfboard Company. His boards are the first available on the market. But with the rise of Nazism, the auspicious, Indian cross takes on an entirely different sense and the logo of the Swastika Surfboard Company starts to become a problem.

1935

After having created the first hollow boards, the American Tom Blake invents the fin, which, placed on the bottom of the surfboard, gives one more stability and makes turning easier. But the fin wouldn't be generally used until the end of the '40s. In Hawaiian Surfboard, a book he also published in 1935, Tom Blake recounts and reflects upon his experience of *he'e nalu*.

A producer of roller skates, Chicago Roller Skate Company, patents an axle system, the truck, pivoting around a vertical axis partially supported by rubber washers. Skateboard trucks are still constructed according to the same principle to this day.

At the end of the '30s, roller skates and the scooter are in fashion. Roller skates are a highly marketed toy, contrary to the scooter, whose grooved wheels are in fact more sophisticated. To make up for their lack of availability, children start constructing their own, which they call *scooter skates*. Scooter skates are constructed from a roller skate cut in half, each piece of which is nailed to the ends of a plank of wood, more often than not a two by four. The steering mechanism, a simple horizontal bar, is affixed to the small, wooden box. Scooter skates quickly become the rage all across the United States. Children soon forego the small wooden box, keeping only the plank of wood and the wheels. This is how the first skateboards are invented.

1956
Humco is the first company to industrially produce skateboards.

After three years of research and experimentation, a surfer from Malibu, David Sweet, markets the first polyurethane foam and polyester resin surfboards.

1957
For more than ten years, a group of young, somewhat beatnik surfers have occupied the beaches in San Onofre and Malibu, just north of Los Angeles. In Malibu, Terry "Tubesteak" Tracy lives in a little cabin that he built on the beach. It is the local hangout of a band of surfers, the most talented of whom is Miki Dora. Tubesteak, Dora and the other *beach bums* have nothing against the arrival of little Kathy Kohner (whom Tubesteak nicknames Gidget, a portmanteau word of *girl* and *midget*), daughter of a writer and Hollywood scriptwriter who is often known to willingly share the contents of her parents' kitchen with the group.

Every night, upon returning home, Kathy Kohner recounts the day's adventures to her parents. Her father, Frederick Kohner, uses the material for a novel entitled Gidget, which is published the same year. Gidget sells 500,000 copies and Life Magazine goes to Malibu to photograph Kathy Kohner and the *Beach Bums*.

Births of Tony Alva and Stacy Peralta.

1959
Roller Derby skateboards appear on the market. The skateboard is also known as the *sidewalk surfboard*. The wheels of these first industrially produced skateboards are metallic cylinders of about 5 cm (2 inches) in diameter and 1 cm (0.4 inches) wide. Roller skate wheels, known as *clay wheels*, would soon replace them. *Clay wheels* are composed of a strange admixture of clay, plastic, paper and a skin of shaved nuts, all of it bonded together with polymer. They put up virtually no resistance to concrete and their life spans rarely go beyond a day.

Although more and more popular, the *sidewalk surfboard* is still considered a toy. Some surfers, however, begin to see them as alternatives to a waveless day and make their own skateboards in the form of mini surfboards made of solid oak.

An expurgated version of Gidget is adapted to the silver screen. Its success is immediate and sets the precedent for the Hollywood genre of the *beach movie*. Hordes of teenagers invade Malibu and end up displacing the *Beach Bums*. Gidget's success coincides with the development of polyurethane foam and polyester resin surfboards of which Hobie and Velzy are the largest manufacturers.

1961
Larry Stevenson, editor in chief of Surf Guide, begins to write articles on skateboarding. He is the first person to publicly associate, in a specialized magazine, surfing and skateboarding. His point of view is still far from producing any unanimity.

In his garage in Santa Monica, Skip Engblom makes his first skateboards by hand.

Birth of Jay Adams.

1962
Val Surf opens in October, in North Hollywood, California. It's the first surf shop situated in a city, far from the beach; it's also the first to sell skateboards. Bill Richards and his two sons order trucks and wheels from the Chicago Roller Skate Company. Then students from the local high school make boards themselves and put them together. In the beginning, sales do not exceed ten boards a week. When they eventually begin to rise, Val Surf joins forces with Hobie Alter, a major surfboard company.

1963
Larry Stevenson founds his own company, Makaha Skateboards. His boards, which he produces in Santa Monica, resemble miniature surfboards. They are between 60 and 80 cm (24 and 32 inches) long and use *clay wheels*. Makaha skateboards cost from 10 to 13 dollars. By the end of the year, Makaha is selling 10,000 skateboards a day.

At the same time, Skee Skate, another company, puts small 3 dollar skateboards with metal wheels on the market. Parents are drawn to the lower prices. The metal wheels seem to them more solid than *clay wheels* while they in fact wear down just as quickly, are slippery and make skateboarding unnecessarily dangerous.

Makaha organizes the first skateboard contest in the schoolyard of the Pier Avenue Junior High School in Hermosa, California. The contest is divided into a freestyle contest, a series of improvised tricks without any obstacles as well as a high jump contest. In the latter, the skater jumps over a suspended bar while his skateboard passes underneath it. A good jump naturally means landing with both feet on the board without losing one's balance. Skateboards are ridden more often than not without shoes.

Still following the surfing model, Makaha sponsors the first team in the history of skateboarding. Skateboarding is clearly not a team sport and the team is to skateboarding what a stable of artists is to a gallery. The sponsors begin by providing skate material for their skaters. According to the capacity of the company and the status of the skater (amateur or professional), the skater eventually earns money (through a monthly salary, by doing *demos* [skate demonstrations] and quite a bit later, by appearing in a magazine). Team Makaha is composed of Squeak Blank (the winner of the Hermosa contest), Danny Bearer, Woody Woodward, Terry Spencer, Steve Tanner and John Fries. Larry Stevenson organizes *demos* throughout California.

Gary Swanson is the first skater to ride an empty swimming pool.

Births of Alan Gelfand and Mike McGill.

1964
Dave and Steve, Baron Hilton's sons, are good surfers and skaters. Through them, their father gets involved with the skateboarding market. Vita Pakt, a fruit juice company which is part of the Hilton empire, contacts Hobie Alter and offers to fund its own skateboard company, Hobie Skateboards. Thus established, Hobie brings together the best surfer-skaters of the time (Hobie Alter recruits them notably from its largest competitor, Makaha). The team

crosses the United States from Los Angeles to New York. Hobie Alter organizes *demos* as well as projections of <u>The Endless Summer</u>, the surf movie that Bruce Brown has just finished and which would quickly become a cult film. The Hobie skaters are some of the first to skate in pools.

With more than 80 other American surfers, Jim Fitzpatrick, from the Dave Sweet Surfboard Team, flies to Biarritz. He arrives with a dozen skateboards in his luggage, giving them away to local surfers.

The first issue of the magazine <u>Quarterly Skateboarder</u> comes out at the end of the year; it is dedicated exclusively to skateboarding. No more than four issues would be published. By the end of 1965, it would have already ceased to exist.

Using a Beach Boys melody, the band Jan and Dean sings "Sidewalk Surfin'"
> Grab your board and go sidewalk surfin' with me…
> Don't be afraid to try the newest sport around
> It's catchin' on in every city and town
> You can do the tricks the surfers do, just try a
> "Quasimodo" or "The Coffin" too […]
> You'll probably wipeout when you first try to shoot the curve […]
>
> Takin' gas in a bush takes a lotta nerve […]
> So get your girl and take her tandem down the street
> Then she'll know you're an asphalt athlete.
> A downhill grade, man, will give you a kick,
> But if the sidewalk's cracked, ya better pull out quick… […]
> (Skateboard with me, why don't you stakeboard with me.)

Birth of Steve Caballero.

1965
Between 1963 and 1965, Makaha's sales reach 4 million dollars. In less than three years, the total sales of skateboards from all the companies combined comes to 50 million dollars. The Hobie Super Surfer, which costs 20 dollars, is a best seller; up to 20,000 are sold a day. Hobie produces its own trucks. They are based on

the Chicago Trucks of the Chicago Roller Company, and they are just a little better. Hobie Alter hears about prototypes of urethane wheels. The skaters on the team quite like them, but Vita Pakt refuses to replace *clay wheels* explaining that the price of skateboards would become too high, and the stock of 20 dollar models, of which a great deal remain, would become useless and unsalable. Skaters would have to wait another 8 years for urethane wheels to hit the market and replace *clay wheels* once and for all.

The International Skateboard Championships in Anaheim, California are broadcast on television. In may the same year, the female skater Pat McGee is featured on the cover of Life Magazine in conjunction with the article "The Craze and The Menace of Skateboards."

In August, following a number of accidents, skateboarding is forbidden in about 20 American cities. The California Medical Association writes in a report that it is a "new medical menace." Local inhabitants and pedestrians already consider it to be a nuisance.

The fourth and final issue of Quarterly Skateboarder comes out at the end of the year.

1966

The first Vans store opens on March 15th at 794 East Broadway in Anaheim, California. The concept of the Van Doren Rubber Company, owned by Van Doren brothers, is to customize your own shoes. Vans offers three models of shoes as well as a large scale of different kinds of fabrics to choose from. A pair is made the same day in a work studio connected to the store.

The first crash of the skateboarding industry occurs. Beginning toward the end of 1965, cancellations of orders take place daily by the hundreds in the offices of Hobie and Makaha. The equivalent of several millions dollars worth of skateboards piles up in their warehouses. The laws against skateboarding are not wholly responsible for young people's loss of interest. The material is still of a very poor quality: beyond the fact that this makes skateboarding more dangerous than it has to be, it impedes any sense of progress. Tricks do not evolve, and skaters get bored.

1965 → 1966

The idea of the skate park has not yet taken root. There are only two in the United States, one in Orange Country, California, and another in Kelso, Washington.

A colleague of the Nouvelle Vague directors, the Quebecois Claude Jutra makes a short, fictional documentary about skateboarding. The original title of the film is Rouli-Roulant (the French-Quebecois word for skateboard), but the title of the English version The Devil's Toy is closer to Jutra's vision. A voice-over (akin to the computer in Jean-Luc Godard's Alphaville, made the year before) presents skateboarding by comparing it to a disease that spreads from city to city. Claude Jutra, who dedicates the film "to all victims of intolerance," shows how children are driven away from public spaces by the forces of order that confiscate their rouli-roulants. The only way they can get their skateboards back is if they agree to crowd into a flat and empty gymnasium and indulge in their pastime in conditions of the utmost safety.

With Skater Dater (which in some ways recalls François Truffaut's The Mischief Makers [1957]), Noel Black wins the grand prize for short films at the 20th Cannes Film Festival. The film follows the leisure-filled days of seven pre-teenage skaters in a small, coastal town in the United States. The innocent harmony of the small group is upset by a new, nascent passion: girls. Noel Black films the movements and attitudes of the skaters with great sensitivity. Even though it is fictional, Skater Dater documents skateboarding in the '60s with first rate quality.

In France, a little late, the magazine Tintin (#916, May 12th, 1966) publishes an article on skateboarding, "Acrobaties pour une planche à roulettes, le Roll' Surf." (Acrobatics for a skateboard, the Roll' Surf). "You all know 'surfing,' this sport imported from America which consists of being carried by a wave until it breaks. For the city person, it seemed a bit difficult to find a patch of water, not to mention some waves. A solution had to be found and "Roll' Surf" seems to be it. A board affixed to four little wheels, set along a longitudinal axis— that's what it looks like. The various possibilities of the skateboard depend entirely on the ability and experience of the "Roll' Surfer." Skate terrain is not hard to come by: a flat, sufficiently unencumbered surface suffices (terraces, covered markets, sidewalks, etc.).

It's a complete sport, very close to skiing, where one finds the same postures and tricks, turns, slaloming, and sudden sharp stops."

Birth of Tommy Guerrero and Rodney Mullen.

1967

In Los Angeles, the amusement park situated on the Pacific Ocean Pier (a pier whose name is often abbreviated as P.O.P.) definitively shuts down. The pier covers The Cove, a little beach on the border between Venice and Santa Monica. The Cove is a secret spot exclusively used by a small group of surfers from Santa Monica. The pylons of the pier, of which certain parts have broken and crumbled, render it particularly dangerous. The beach is by no means paradisiacal; it's the confluence of the ocean and a dump. The surfers share the spot with junkies, hobos and other local pariahs. The ruins of buildings that surround The Cove are covered with graffiti, a notable example of which is the famous "Locals Only." Much more than the beaches of Venice or South Santa Monica, and already far from the pristine beaches of Malibu, The Cove is the spot that best symbolizes a generation of atypical surfers who could almost come from a novel by Kerouac or Bukowski.

1968

Jeff Ho and Skip Engblom are part of The Cove surfer clique. They open a work-surf shop in Santa Monica called, The Jeff Ho Zephyr Productions Surf Shop, known more simply as Zephyr Shop. Jeff Ho is a noted and innovative *shaper* (a surfboard maker, literally, he who shapes the boards). Craig R. Stecyk, a local artist and friend of Jeff Ho and Skip Engblom, paints Zephyr's unusual boards. Very influenced by gang graffiti, the aesthetic of customized cars and Harley Davidson motorcycles (the famous Route 66 ends in Santa Monica), Craig R. Stecyk adapts urban culture to surfboards.

Births of Tony Hawk and Mark Gonzales.

1969

Makaha puts together a new team, which features a handful of skaters from the San Bernardo Valley, one of the last bastions of skating in the down years. Brad and Bruce Logan, Ty Page, Torger Johnson, Danny Bearer, the Hilton Brothers, Tommy Ryan and

John Fries are the first skaters to skate the banks that populate a number of Santa Monica schoolyards. They borrow heavily from the language of surfing and transcribe its movements to asphalt. Thus, to do a "frontside" turn is to turn on the bank while facing it, while "backside" is to turn with one's back to the bank. Little by little, the Makaha team starts doing demos again.

Larry Stevenson, the now famous founder of Makaha, patents the *kicktail*, which is to say, it occurs to him to raise the back of the board, the tail, so that it might be easier to use it as a point of leverage with to lift up the front of the board. He would never manage to earn any royalties on his invention; a tribunal even considered the invention to be a given. Until that time, skateboards had been completely flat. Pivoting on the back wheels (i.e., "kickturns"), the *kicktail* makes turning easier. Different from "carving" (wherein the skater turns via the suppleness of the trucks with all four wheels on the ground), the kickturn does not come from surfing. This basic trick is considered the first sign of emancipation of skateboarding from surfing.

Near Los Angeles, Pat "Muckus" Mullus discovers Mount Baldy Pipeline, a giant water pipeline that was part of a drainage system in the event of violent storms. The tube is around 4.5 meters (15 feet) in diameter and a 150 meters (500 feet) long. Skaters see this cylinder as a double wave and take it over immediately. At the end of the '70s, the Mount Baldy Pipeline would be renamed The Badlands.

Birth of Natas Kaupas whose name is Lithuanian; read backwards, his first name inevitably stirs up a bit of controversy.

1970
Jay Adams is 8 years old, and, in addition to having a specialized, fiberglass workshop, his stepfather runs a surfboard rental stand in Venice Beach. Tony Alva is four years older than him, and like him, lives in a part of Santa Monica renamed Dogtown by the local surfers. Alva and Adams are the youngest surfers of The Cove. They skate as well, making their boards out of solid oak as in the old days. Following the suggestions of older surfers, they go to the Paul Revere Junior High School whose schoolyard is boardeded by a long asphalt bank that is about 4 meters (13 feet) high.

Births of Jason Lee and Mike Vallely. Frankie Hill is born the year after, 1971.

1972

Frank Nasworthy goes to see one of his friends whose father runs a small company that specializes in urethane (Creative Urethane), a material developed from petrol in Germany in the '30s. In a corner of the workshop, he discovers a stock of wheels destined for the roller skate manufacturer, Roller Sports. His father's friend gives about 30 more or less defective wheels to Nasworthy. The enthusiasm of the skaters who roadtest these wheels is unanimous. Urethane gets much better traction, makes the wheels more supple and wears down a lot less quickly than *clay wheels*. But Creative Urethane can't sell another client's product. Frank Nasworthy designs the first urethane wheel conceived especially for skateboards, the Cadillac Wheel, then sells it to local Los Angeles surf shops. The urethane wheel is largely responsible for giving skateboarding its second wave of popularity.

Birth of Ed Templeton.

1973

Through Jay Adams and Tony Alva, Skip Engblom discovers the Cadillac Wheel. Bahne Skateboards is the largest skateboard company, and Engblom tells himself that it must be possible to create better boards. He asks Jay Adams' stepfather, Kent Sherwood, who becomes associated with Zephyr Shop, for help. Zephyr skates are made in a kind of plastic, which is colored, flexible and solid at the same time. The young skaters in the neighborhood go crazy for them.

Richard Novak, Doug Haut and Jay Shuirman are *shapers* associated under the name of NHS (their initials). They work for the Santa Cruz Surf Shop. Since they have a lot of extra fiberglass, they decide to begin creating decks, and found Santa Cruz Skateboards.

The young skaters of Dogtown discover a number of empty pools in some of the wealthiest neighborhoods of Los Angeles, especially in Beverly Hills. Most Californian pools are shaped like kidneys and the walls transition from the vertical to the horizontal. They are entirely constructed in raw concrete with the exception of tiles located on the vertical part of the wall (the vert) just under the edge of the pool, which skaters refer to as the *lip*. Thanks to their urethane wheels Tony Alva, Jay Adams, Stacy Peralta, Bob Biniak and their buddies are quickly able to hit the tiles, and to therefore to skate the vertical part of the transition. They call this trick "blue tiling" in reference to the color of the tiles (most often blue). "Off the lip" is another trick that consists of turning and letting a wheel go beyond the lip of the pool. When trucks become wider, the "off the lip" would become the "grind" in which the back truck hits and grinds the edge of the coping or lip of the pool.

1974
The Cadillac Wheel is extremely popular. It is 49 mm (around 2 inches) in diameter and 30 mm (1.2 inches) wide. Roller Sports, which until now limited itself to the roller skate market, realizes that the market for skateboards is not negligible and buys all of Creative Urethane's production. Roller Sports partners with Bahne Skateboards, which then becomes Bahne Cadillac. During this time, George Powell, an aeronautic engineer, starts making decks for his son.

Like Paul Revere Junior High School, the schools of Brentwood, Bellagio, Kenter Canyon and Mar Vista are constructed at different levels on the side of hills. Their schoolyards aren't separated by simple little walls, but rather by long inclines of varying heights. These asphalt waves become veritable, improvised skate parks. From 1973 to 1975, the Paul Revere Junior High school, located about 8 km (5 miles) from Dogtown in the neighborhood of Pacific Palisades, is the most popular. The police make appearances there with increasingly regularity and skateboarding becomes impossible just as at Bellagio Elementary School. The skaters migrate to Kenter Canyon Elementary, 6 km (4 miles) east of Paul Revere. The school is constructed so high on the side of a mountain that the police rarely go there. From 1975 to 1978, between 50 and 100 skaters frequent the spot daily. At the same time, skaters rediscover the giant pipeline of Mount Baldy.

Birth of Danny Way.

1975

There are an estimated 2 million skaters in Southern California.

While the Cadillac Wheel is equipped with a free ball-bearing system, NHS puts a wheel with a precision ball-bearing system on the market: the Road Rider. Nasworthy becomes victim of his own success; with a stock too large to dump, he can't permit himself to change his ball-bearing system. Thus NHS, Sims and Kryptonics' wheels outsell the Cadillac Wheel.

The appearance of Tracker trucks comes right after the Bennett Hijacker, which turns better, but has a reputation for being less solid. The kingpin (the vertical bolt upon which the rubbers are placed) does not go beyond the horizontal axis of the truck, and this allows for much easier grinding. The company 3M commercializes the first rolls of "grip tape," pieces of self-adhesive sandpaper specifically conceived to adhere to the top of skateboards so that skaters have better traction. Grip tape exists in three colors, black, red and blue.

Jeff Ho and Skip Engblom create the Zephyr Team which brings together the best young skater-surfers of Dogtown, the Z-Boys: Tony Alva, Jay Adams, Stacy Peralta, Bob Biniak, Shogo Kubo, Paul Constantineau, Wes Humpston, Jim Muir, Alan Sarlo, Nathan Pratt, Wentzle Ruml, Cris Dawson, Chris Cahill and Peggy Oki, the only girl of the group.

For the past several years, surfboards have been getting smaller. They are now 2 meters (6.5 feet) long. Shortboards replace longboards little by little and alter the way people surf. A more physical and dynamic style of surfing appears at the same time, given that the shorter boards allow for very tight turns. The young, Hawaiian surfer Larry Bertlemann is one of the first *shortboarders* to touch the wave with his hand. After seeing a Hal Jepsen film, Super Session, Larry Bertlemann becomes the Z-Boys' idol, who imitate his style and tricks on the ground. By making their wheels slide, they learn how to make sudden turns. On the banks in the schoolyards, they invent the "Bert," a sharp turn with the body really low and a hand placed on the ground, upon which they pivot.

In addition to surfing, Paul Constantineau and Bod Biniak ski. The underground influence of skiing upon skateboarding can be found, for example, in the slalom, the descent (what one often calls the *down-hill*) and generally speaking, a love of pure speed.

The Bahne Cadillac Internationals, a large skateboard contest, takes place in Del Mar on the 26th and the 27th of April. Billy Bahne, the director of Bahne Skateboards, has a slalom run built in wood that is 45 meters (145 feet) long, 9 meters (29.5 feet) wide and 4 meters (13 feet) high. The freestyle contest takes place on a platform of varnished wood, a rather poor terrain for skaters used to the schoolyards. This is where the Z-Boys unveil their tricks borrowed from shortboarding. Compared to the Z-Boys, the Hobie/Makaha generation of skaters (Ty Page, Torger Johnson...) are stiff and immobile, their tricks often closer to gymnastics than to surfing (hand stands, 360s, balancing on the back or front wheels...). They are tricksters, good skaters who master technical tricks. The Z-Boys, on the other hand, seek fluidity, speed and style. The judges find it difficult to judge the Zephyr Team; their tricks still don't have names. Peggy Oki nevertheless wins the women's freestyle. Jay Adams and Tony Alva respectively take third and fourth in the men's freestyle.

The Zephyr team doesn't last long. Kent Sherwood, who no longer gets along with Jeff Ho, founds his own company called EZ. The new team consists of Jay Adams, Paul Cullen and Marty Grimes. In the space of a few months, the Z-Boys have become stars worth their weight in gold and the biggest companies snatch them. Tony Alva and Bob Biniak join Logan Earth Ski. Wentzle Ruml takes an offer from Makaha, while Paul Constantineau and Stacy Peralta skate for Gordon & Smith. In less than two years, the Stacy Peralta Warptail by Gordon & Smith, a board laminated in wood and fiberglass, sells more than one hundred thousand. In order to meet this demand, Kent Sherwood is forced to subcontract. But the factory he uses does not respect his fabrication techniques and EZ's decks become very poor quality. Towards the end of the year, Sherwood takes things back under his control and EZ becomes Z-Flex.

The magazine <u>Quarterly Skateboarder</u> starts back up with the simple name <u>Skateboarder</u>. After the second issue, and under the pseudonym of John Smythe, Craig Stecyk's articles and photos help create the myth of Dogtown and the Z-Boys. His first article, "Aspect of the Downhill Slide," features one of the most quoted observations in the history of skateboarding: "Two hundred years of American technology has unwittingly created a massive cement playground of unlimited potential. But it was the mind of 11 years olds that could see that potential."

Jay Adams, Paul Constantineau and Tony Alva spend the winter in Hawaii, where they surf and start skating a *ditch*, a concrete water evacuation conduit, which would quickly become famous under the moniker of Wallos.

Jack Graham and John O'Malley are neighbors. After having seen police arrest some young skaters in the street, they consider the possibility of constructing spaces exclusively built for skateboarding. Everything gathers serious momentum when one of Graham's son's friends is hit by a car and dies. They conceive and create the Carlsbad Skatepark in California, which opens in the summer. Carlsbad is composed of *snake runs* (winding paths reminiscent of bobsleigh runs, though much larger), bowls (spaces similar to pools, but with softer transitions and, at the time, without vert) and flat spaces reserved for freestyle skating. Skate City opens one week before Carlsbad in Port Orange, Florida.

Spyder Wills and Greg Weaver make <u>Downhill Motion</u>, a 36-minute documentary about skateboarding in which they show all of its facets: freestyle (featuring Russ Howell, the skater-gymnast), street, ditches and schoolyards with their banks, the Escondido reservoir, California, whose form is somewhere between a bowl and a ditch, pools (featuring the ex-Z-Boys), the full pipe in Mount Baldy, the slalom, the high jump, riding a skateboard and being pulled by one or several dogs, the all-terrain skateboard (on grass or dirt), down-hill which is done standing as well as crouching or even laying down (featuring the future record holder for speed, Guy Grundy).

In France, some skaters are already paid and travel from city to city to do demos. Skateboarding seeks to establish itself as a sport. In organized groups, young skaters do the high jump, the slalom, and free style skating.

Births of Mike Carroll, Eric Koston and Daewon Song.

1976

In January, a third truck company appears on the market, Gullwing. Following the advice of his father who is a woodworker, Willi Winkel, a young Canadian skater-skier, creates the first skateboard deck in laminated maple. Beyond the fact that this process renders the board both hard and flexible at the same time, this technique makes it easier to bend and raise the tail. Plastic, fiberglass and carbon would be gradually rendered obsolete by seven-ply maple, of which skateboards are still made to this day. Willi Winkel starts producing skateboards and founds a company. Lonnie Toft, a professional skateboarder who is sponsored by Sims and who is passing through Canada, meets Winkel and shows him his design for a very wide skateboard, which would require four trucks and eight wheels. Taken by the idea, Winkel cuts it for him immediately. Upon his return to the United States, Lonnie Toft has the Sims logo printed on his eight-wheel deck, signs up for a contest and wins it. The demand for the board is immediate and Sims makes an order with Willi Winkel.

At the same time, George Powell creates the Quicksilver ProSlalom for Sims, an aluminum and fiberglass deck destined to rival Gordon & Smith's Fiberflex. Makaha puts Radial, a 100% nylon shoe, on the market. Much more popular, the Van Doren brothers' new model, the Vans Era, is conceived with the collaboration of Tony Alva and Stacy Peralta.

Drainage Ditches (which are generally abbreviated as ditches, or just ditch, dropping the *drainage*) are long concrete inclines created for the drainage of water in the event of flash floods, whose banked walls recall the now famous schools in Los Angeles. In just a few years they have become veritable readymade skate parks. In Albuquerque, New Mexico, skaters gather by the hundreds and the ditch begins to resemble a ski run in the middle of the desert. On the Big Island of Hawaii, Wallos becomes a world-famous spot where it is not rare to come across Larry Bertlemann, shoeless on his skateboard.

Due to a major drought, the use of water is limited in California. In Los Angeles, one is no longer allowed to water one's garden and pools become empty: a godsend for the new wave of pool skaters. Techniques for locating pools multiply: with Jay Adams standing on the roof of his pickup truck, Stacy Peralta drives around the streets of Beverly Hills. In certain real estate agencies, the ex-Z-Boys find addresses of uninhabited mansions. A controversial anecdote recounts how Jay Adams and Shogo Kubo would go so far as to pay a pilot to fly over certain neighborhoods. When the pools are not completely empty, a pump linked to a generator allows for speedy drainage. The sessions are often quite rapid (sometimes not going beyond ten minutes), with skaters taking turns to keep an eye out for the police, disappearing at the first peal of a siren.

Two new skateparks open in Florida, in Cocoa (Paved Wave) and Pensacola. Others are built in different states, notably in Rhode Island (Yogoo Valley in Slocum) and in Southern California (Fun Land in Myrtle Beach). Skaters are quick to criticize these first generation skate parks. Vert becomes the preferred terrain of skaters and skate parks offer very little in the way of spaces based on Californian pools. Craig Stecyk complains about them in "State of the Art," an article published at the end of the year in the magazine <u>Skateboarder</u>: "Skateparks are frequently touted as the future of skateboarding. While fine for what they are, the parks in general have so far failed to surpass many quality, already extant skate spots. Have you yet seen a park as radical as the best pools? [...] The more advanced parks will offer the more advanced terrains."

<u>Go for it</u>, Paul Rapp's film, which was produced by Hal Jepsen (the director of <u>Super Session</u>) is a 92-minute documentary dedicated to surfing, skateboarding and skiing. It also features footage of hang gliding, rafting and rock climbing. This film is of a particularly important historical interest: barely two years after <u>Super Session</u> came out, Tony Alva, Jay Adams and the ex-Z-Boys feature in the movie with their idol, the surfer Larry Bertlemann (who can be seen skating Wallos in Hawaii). As in <u>Downhill Motion</u>, skateboarding is represented in all its diversity: pools, ditches, schoolyards, skate parks (with very beautiful images of Carlsbad), downhill, freestyle, and high jump. The film even shows a bit of "gorilla grip," a kind of jump that couldn't be done

unless one was barefoot given that one had to grip the ends of the deck with one's toes in order to do it. As impressive as this may seem, some skaters even managed to pull off "Frontside 360 gorilla grips."

Guy Grundy enters the Guinness Book of World Records for the highest speed on a skateboard: 80 km/h (about 50 miles per hour).

Births of Brian Anderson, Rob Dyrdek, Geoff Rowley and Jamie Thomas.

1977

George Powell founds Powell Corporation. He brings out the Quicktail, a more rigid deck, made of maple and aluminum, created for freestyle as well as for vert. He also works on a double radial wheel in white urethane, The Bones.

Raymond H. Losi is the founder of Variflex. The company becomes one of the most important around the end of the '70s.

Santa Cruz brings out the 5 ply, a deck constituted by five thin layers of laminated maple.

Wes Humston and Jim Muir officially found Dogtown Skateboards, even though they had already started to create, paint and sell their own decks in 1975. A piece of graffiti by Craig Stecyk, the "Dogtown Cross," becomes their logo. From 1978, Dogtown would be the first company to print a drawing on their boards (rather than a simple logo).

Tony Alva becomes world champion. Soon after his victory, he leaves Logan Earth Ski to create his company, Alva Skateboards. His first ad appears in the December issue of Skateboarder.

Vans brings out the famous Style 38, better known under the Skate Hi, a high top shoe, padded around the ankle. In order to promote Skate Hi, Vans signs a contract with Stacy Peralta, who becomes the first skater to receive a monthly paycheck ($300, which now corresponds to roughly $900) from the shoe company.

Mike Rector invents fall protection, known as pads, such as knee pads and elbow pads, which come with a hard shell. Until that time, skaters had used volleyball knee pads. The possibility of safer falls through the invention of knee slides (when they fall, skaters seek to cushion the impact by sliding down the transition on their knee pads) will help promote the more rapid invention of new tricks.

Rick Blackhard and the Thatcher brothers hear about the Glory Hole, a dam built in the '50s in Northern California. They go and discover a *full-pipe* of roughly 9 meters (29.5 feet) in diameter. In order to get to it, one must cross a small lake in a boat. Again in northern California, in the vicinity of Palo Alto, skaters discover the full-pipes of Ameron Plant, a nuclear power plant under construction. New full pipes are located in the Arizona desert, between Lake Pleasant and Biscuit Flat. They are part of the Central Arizona Project, a 541 kilometers (336 miles) diversion canal project initiated in 1973 by the appropriately named Barry Goldwater. Warren Bolster's (the editor in chief of Skateboarder magazine) photos of these sessions are of a striking beauty. The images are quite close to Nancy Holt's documentary photos of one of her Land Art pieces, entitled Sun Tunnels, created the year before (1976) which is comprised of four concrete cylinders 2.75 meters (9 feet) in diameter.

Londoners begin to skate the South Bank located along the Thames under the Hayward Gallery. In Paris, the Eiffel Tower's ponds are emptied and provide skaters with a taste of Californian skateparks.

A dozen new skateparks open in Florida and California. Skater-Cross (Reseda, California), Concrete Wave (Anaheim, California) and Solid Surf (Fort Lauderdale, Florida) are equipped, like Carlsbad, with long *snake runs*. Entrepreneurs possess a poor knowledge of skateboarding and do not understand that the majority of skaters have no interest in terrains based on bobsledding or motocross. Skaters hope to find pools, ditches, and full-pipes in parks. This goes on to engender a second generation of skateparks of which the most emblematic is Pipeline, in Upland, in the San Bernadino Valley, California. The full-pipe that lends its name and identity to Pipeline is constructed after the giant tunnel of Mount Baldy. It is 6 meters (20 feet) high and 12 meters (40 feet) long, and opens up into a bowl that it is 9 meters (29 feet) in diameter and 3.65 meters (12 feet) deep. The second bowl is even bigger, 12 meters (39 feet) wide and 4.6 meters (15 feet) deep, featuring a section that it is *over-vert* (a part of the transition that curls over itself, as in the letter C). The play of words on the name of the park is quite witty and echoes the culture of skateboarding. First of all, a pipeline is a concrete pipe. Surfers referred to the curled over, interior space known to happen in waves as a "tube." In Hawaii, one of the most famous surf spots in the history of surfing is known as Pipeline. The names of numerous skateparks refer to the aquatic origins of skateboarding, such as Concrete Wave, Paced Wave, and Solid Surf. Pipeline is a kind of double homage, to the ocean and concrete, to wave forms as much to as to those of industry. Before Pipeline, Longwood skatepark in Florida is the first to possess a full pipe (3.6 meters, 12 feet in diameter).

The first French skatepark, conceived by Jean-François Heuty, is inaugurated in Saint-Jean-de-Luz on the 14th of July. It is a 3000 square meter (32,000 sq foot) park with about 9000 entries a month. But the appearance of cracks and other problems would soon render it useless. Parallel to concrete skateparks, wooden constructions make their debut, most often in the form of half-pipes without any flat bottom, platform or coping (the metal or plastic tube that would soon replace the concrete lip of pools in these new kinds of construction), the ancestors of ramps such as we know them today. Some people even began to construct quarter-pipes, as depicted in Glen E. Friedman's photos of the Oakmont Drive Ramp.

The ex-Z-Boys gather during the famous Dog Bowls sessions also documented by Friedman. The Dog Bowl is a private pool situated in a rich neighborhood in Santa Monica. Dino, a young skater diagnosed with cancer, asks his father to empty their pool so his friends can come skate it. It is at this Dog Bowl that Tony Alva pulls off the first "frontside air," a trick (from the general family of "aerials") that consists of turning in the air above the pool coping while keeping one's skateboard on one's feet by holding it with one's hand.

At roughly the same time, far from the flashes of cameras in a skatepark in Florida, Alan Gelfand, nicknamed "Ollie" by his friends, invents a movement that allows him to jump over the coping without holding his skateboard with his hand. The trick soon takes on the name "Ollie pop." It is without a doubt the most important trick in the history of skateboarding. Photos of Alan Gelfand doing the Ollie wouldn't appear in Skateboarder for more than another year. The "ollie pop" is mastered by very few skaters in 1979.

Among another register, Nathan Pratt is known for his vertiginous *gaps*, which is to say, clearing expanses of stairs or other kinds of gaps, without actually ollieing (which, in fact, has yet to even be incorporated into street skating) by virtue of sheer speed.

Pepsi-Cola organizes tours of skate demos throughout the U.S., which can be seen as an indicator of how popular skateboarding has become. Just as in airplanes before each takeoff, the show starts by reminding all the skaters of certain safety precautions they should observe while skating. The main attraction of Pepsi Pro *demos* is without a doubt the transparent, Plexiglas half-pipe on which Dave and Paul Hackett do "airs," their feet stuck to their skateboards with Velcro.

In the magazine Skateboarder, Craig Stecyk questions Wentzle Ruml about his injuries; the subject thereafter seems to become quite popular, with skaters often exhibiting their injuries like trophies. Ruml responds that he has already chipped three teeth, dislocated an elbow and split a lip, which required 16 stitches.

In Florida, on the 1st of January in 1977, the father of the young Rodney Mullen finally gives his son a skateboard. He makes it very clear to Rodney that at the sign of the least injury, skateboarding is over. By the end of the year, The Inland Surf Shop becomes the Rodney Mullen's first sponsor.

While Skateboarder magazine becomes a monthly, the first issue of Skateboard comes out in France. It is also the same year as the publication of a single issue of Skate France Magazine, which becomes Skate France International in 1978.

The first French skateboarding contest is organized in Bayonne. One year after Germany and Great Britain, skateboarding explodes in France.

Birth of Marc Johnson.

1978

There are an estimated 20 million skateboarders in the United States. Some estimates go as far as 40 million. Given that the figure doubles, these numbers are highly unreliable. Suffice it to say the number of skateboarders is immense. Skateboarder magazine has a million readers. The United States Consumer Product Safety Committee registers 325,000 skateboard-related accidents this year.

Stacy Peralta goes into business with George Powell. The Powell Corporation becomes Powell Peralta, which would go on to be, along with Santa Cruz and Vision, one of the most important skateboard companies of the '80s. The young Ray "Bones" Rodriguez is their first professional skater. Vernon Courtland conceives the graphics of his *pro-model* (this is when professional skaters have a personal pro-model named after them, and earn a percentage from the sale of each deck): the hands of a skeleton holding a sword in front of its skull. Skaters go crazy for it. Thanks to Vernon Courtland, Powell Peralta finds a visual identity, a bestiary of skeletons and fantastic animals associated with each skater.

After creating Ermico, and designing several models of trucks without success, Fausto Vitello, Eric Swenson and John Solomine go into business with NHS and launch Independent Trucks. Tested by Rick Blackhart and Steve Olson, they quickly become popular. The team features the best skaters of the new generation: Blackhart, Olson, Steve Alba, Duane Peters, Bobby Valdez and Brad Brown. By the end of the year, Independent accounts for 50% of all truck sales. Duane Peters, Steve Olson and the Alba brothers (Steve known as "Salba" and Micky, known as "Malba") ride for Santa Cruz, NHS's company. Along with Rick Blackhart, they are the first skaters to go punk: blue jeans, leather vests and Chuck Taylor Converses.

At the beginning of the year, boards are still really narrow, between 15 and 17 cm (6 and 7 inches) wide. The widest model of Independent Trucks, the Superwide 131 is 131 mm (5.16 inches) wide. These developments, as well as the kicktail, are what differentiate these skateboards from boards of the '60s. After the success of the Lonnie Toft model (Sims), decks by the biggest companies, Dogtown, Sims, Santa Cruz, Powell Peralta and finally

Alva, go up to a width of 25 cm (about 10 inches); the length stabilizes between 75 and 80 cm (27.5 and 31 inches). Independent creates two new truck models, the FW 151 (Fucking Wide 151 mm – 5.94 inches) and the MFW169 (Mother Fucking Wide 169 mm – 6.65 inches).

Skaters continue to complain about second-generation skateparks. Their surfaces are not always smooth enough; they slow you down and shred up your skin like sandpaper when you fall. Skaters would like to have coping on the pools, because it facilitates certain tricks like "grinds" and "airs." Skaters get involved with supervising a third generation of skateparks, the most successful of which are Skate in the Shade (Tempe, Arizona), Winchester (San Jose, California), Cherry Hill (New Jersey), Marina del Rey (Santa Monica, California), Endless Wave (Oxnard, California), Surf De Earth (Vista, California) and Del Mar Skate Ranch (San Diego, California), which features an exact replica of a famous pool known as the Kona Bowl.

Marina del Rey Skatepark, which is inaugurated on the 18th of November, is situated in the heart of Dogtown, in Santa Monica. Two famous pools, the Dog Bowl and The Keyhole, are re-created there; the park is known for its *vert*.

Cherry Hill, in New Jersey, is one of the first indoor skate parks. In addition to its four bowls, one of which is the famous Egg Bowl, and which is more than 3.5 meters (11.5 feet) deep, Cherry Hill is known for its long concrete *half-pipe* and its *over-vert* section. Along with Marina del Rey, it is Tony Alva and Jay Adams' favorite park.

Between 1978 and 1979, in order to compete, the big, second generation skateparks modernize. Skate City (Whittier) builds a Keyhole similar to that of Marina del Rey as well as a *full-pipe*. A contractor, which specializes in pools, builds the famous combi-pool: an imbrication of three pools of different sizes and forms. The largest two are 4 meters (13 feet) deep and 9 meters (29.5 feet) wide. The first bowl is circular, the second is squared with rounded corners, and the third is separated in two by a roll-in.

Skateparks are no longer exclusive to the United States: they are made all over the world, notably in Brazil, Argentina, Germany, England and France.

On the site of an old slaughterhouse, La Villette skatepark is inaugurated in Paris on the 19th of May. Its long snake-run brings to mind the first generation of American skateparks. Conceived by Raymond Baudier, Pierre Gallo and Michel Londinsky, it cost almost 1.5 million francs to construct. Use was paid for by the hour. A week later, a second skatepark is inaugurated in the region of Paris, Béton Hurlant (Howling Concrete), on the island of Saint Germain in Issy-les-Moulineaux. Like La Villette, Béton Hurlant is constructed with sprayed concrete, but unlike the former, a finishing layer is applied by hand. The *half-pipe*, which is 6 meters (20 feet) wide and 15 meters (49 feet) long, is a perfect copy of Skatopia's *half-pipe* (the Buena Park skatepark in California, opened in 1977) while the 3 bowls (respectively 2.5 meters or 8 feet, 3.5 meters or 11 feet and 4 meters deep or 13 feet) are replicas of those of Endless Wave in Oxnard. Béton Hurlant also has a wooden *half-pipe*, it is a more "modern" skatepark than La Villette.

Another concrete skatepark opens in Brittany, not far from Lorient. Smaller than the ones at La Villette and Issy-les-Moulineaux, it is comprised of a *half-pipe*, a *snake-run* and a bowl that is around 3 meters (10 feet) deep.

The third contest of the Hester Series (a circuit specific to bowls and *vert*) takes place at Ride On Skatepark in Newark, in northern California. It is the most important one of the year; many skaters and new tricks are revealed there. Rick Blackhart, Steve Olson, Duane Peters, Steve Alba and his brother Micky skate in Dogtown style, fast and hard. Rick Blackhart is the first to skate the platform on tops of bowls; he turns "backside" out of the bowl ("backside roll out") rides along the coping, and then goes back in ("backside roll in"). During the finals, Blackhart creates a stir by doing a "frontside roll-out/roll-in." Bobby Valdez pulls off one of the first "inverts" in the history of skateboarding (an "aerial" during which a skater places his hand on the coping, and thus inverting his body so that his feet are in the air, before going back in) and barely takes first place (he and Blackhart are initially announced as tied). Just like del Mar in 1975, the two great families of skateboarding are represented: on one side *riders*, fast and powerful skaters who are more interested in style than difficult tricks, and *tricksters*, who focus on the complexity of maneuvers.

Among the numerous tricks invented this year are the "frontside rock n' roll," the "layback grind" and the "alley oop." Eddie Elguera is the inventor of the "frontside rock 'n' roll": once at the top of the transition, he taps the middle underside of his skateboard against the coping, and then turns around, and goes back into the bowl "frontside" (with the bowl at his back). The "layback grind" consists of grinding the back truck against the coping while the skater leans back, placing a hand on the lip at the same time. Finally, the "alley oop" is a kind of contrary "aerial," going out of the bowl "backside" into the air, the skater turns and comes down "frontside" (or the opposite), which necessitates a 270 degree rotation.

Rodney Mullen wins his first freestyle contest in Florida. Steve Olson is voted *Skater of the Year* by the readers of Skateboarder magazine. He is also the overall winner of the Hester Series.

Tony Alva stars in Skateboard, an unsuccessful full-length feature film made by Universal Studios.

Four specialized magazines come out in France: Skate Magazine, Skate France International, Skatin' and Super Skateboard. Trocadéro bleu citron also comes out; a film by Michael Schock in which Anny Duperey plays a mother trying to convince a politician that skateboarding is a fantastic thing to do.

Birth of Andrew Reynolds.

1979
Following the lead of Dogtown Skateboards, all the skateboard companies begin to print drawings on the bottom of their decks. So that skaters have better traction on boards, Santa Cruz, Alva and Variflex start producing concave decks. Tim Puimarta, who works for NHS, develops printing techniques applicable to convex surfaces, allowing graphics to be screen printed on the undersides of this new generation of decks.

Sims brings out Steve Rocco's pro-model, the best freestyler at the time. Just after being elected *Skater of the Year* by the readers of Skateboarder magazine, Stacy Peralta retires from professional skateboarding and establishes the Bones Brigade, which is, along with the Z-Boys, the most famous skate team in the history of skateboarding. Alan Gelfand, Steve Cabellero and Mike McGill join Ray Rodriguez on the team. Tim Scroggs, who lives in Florida like Gelfand, is the only freestyler. He would have a great influence upon Rodney Mullen (who takes first place this year at Oceanside in California, the most important amateur contest there is). At the time, Rodney Mullen is sponsored by Walker Skateboards, a company based in Florida. Tim Scroggs talks to Stacy Peralta about Mullen.

Skaters begin to attach small rails to the bottom of their skateboards, which gives them a better grip on boards when doing "airs." The rails that Paul Schmitt makes are either in wood or urethane. Alan Gelfand and Mike McGill give him a suggestion to make them in a material that slides, allowing "rockslides" and "lipslides" (tricks which consist of sliding the bottom of your board along the coping). Paul Schmitt discovers a UHMW polyethylene, a particularly hard and resistant plastic material. He cuts and puts holes in the rails at the wood shop of his university, then packages them in his parents' living room. His Schmitt Stix become very popular, and it would not be long before they are distributed all over the world by Vision (a new company associated with Sims).

At that moment a whole bunch of plastic accessories appear on the market, which are meant to protect the tail, the nose, and the trucks. *Lappers*, for example, are placed on the back truck. These are little slanted pieces of plastic which, in addition to protecting the kingpin screw during "grinds," theoretically prevent the truck from getting stuck on the coping (known as a "hang-up"). Aside from rails, the existence of these various pieces of plastic would be short-lived and would eventually only be used on low quality, plywood skateboards sold in major department stores.

There are now more than 400 skateparks in the United States, but some begin to shut down. Investors spent too much money and revenues are slow to come. The spaces are used for more lucrative enterprises. Accidents multiply and the number of insurance investigators that parks must hire due to parents' complaints is too high. Bulldozers raze Béton Hurlant before summer. La Villette skatepark closes. Over the summer, the most diehard skaters jump the fence to skate the *snake-run*; as for the bowl, it is full of water and detritus, and therefore unskateable.

Turning Point Ramp is a *full-pipe* built in Plexiglas on a metal armature in the form of a capsule. With a similar construction, Duane Peters fulfills the dream of every skateboarder since the discovery of giant pipes. By gaining enough speed in the largest part of the capsule, Duane Peters, a true disciple of the daredevil Evel Knievel, manages to generate enough velocity necessary to do a complete revolution, his head upside down, in the smallest section. This acrobatic act repeated about ten times would nevertheless earn him a fractured collarbone.

Stacy Peralta sends the photographer James Cassimus to Florida to document Alan Gelfand's "ollie." A sequence is published in Skateboarder and the trick is finally "discovered."

The popularity of skateboarding decreases. Skateboarder magazine no longer covers it in all its diversity, but concentrates rather on pools and skateparks. The magazine reduces the image of the skater to that of a *vert-rider*. Skateboarding becomes elitist; many feel excluded and give it up. Despite their high numbers, skateparks are not easily accessible for everyone (geographically and financially), pools even less so. These forms of skateboarding are difficult and dangerous for beginners who no longer dare put their feet on a skateboard, turning instead to BMX or roller skates.

1980

BMX and roller skaters are the trend. For skateboarding, it's the beginning of a new down period, which would last two years. From August on, Skateboarder becomes Action Now, a magazine featuring articles on skateboarding, surfing, BMXing and rock music. The great American skateparks close, one after another.

Laws do not protect park owners against the complaints of parents of young, injured skaters. The skateboard industry suffers from this decline considerably. In only a year, the number of professional skaters (more or less paid by their sponsors) drops from 175 to about 15.

At the age of 13, Rodney Mullen beats Steve Rocco (six years older than him) and takes first place in the most important freestyle contest of the year (at Oasis Skatepark in San Diego) and then to turns pro for Powell Peralta. He has the song "Psycho Killer" by The Talking Heads played during his *run*.

In the penultimate issue of Skateboarder, the June issue, the first photo of 11 years old Christian Hosoï is published: a "frontside ollie" in one of the bowls at Marina del Rey, where his father is manager. Devo records the video for "Freedom of Choice" in this same skatepark. Dave Andrecht, Jay Smith and Eddie Elguera all star in it.

Skateboard Madness comes out, a film written and directed by Julian Pena Jr and produced again by Hal Jepsen. Essentially made in 1978, the film comes out too late; the tricks and spots in it are already dated. Skateboard Madness nevertheless remains a film of anthological importance; Stacy Peralta, Gregg Ayres and Dan Smith's appearances are all impressive, while even more impressive is Kent Senatore on the Turning Point Ramp, a Plexiglas *full-pipe*, which is inclined and closed on one side, in which Senatore manages to pull off "loops" (complete turns to the point of going upside down). The last sequence, which covers the *full-pipes* in the Arizona desert, is of a breathtaking beauty.

Birth of Chris Haslam.

1981

Fausto Vitello, one of the owners of Hermico/Independent associated with NHS, inaugurates the magazine Thrasher, whose first issue comes out in January. Thrasher is the first magazine created entirely and edited by skaters. The first editorial encourages readers to recapture the spirit before the skate parks, the time when skateboarding meant the discovery and use of new terrains.

Powell Peralta brings out the pro-models of Jay Smith, Alan Gelfand, Mike McGill, Steve Caballero, and Rodney Mullen. A piece of graffiti by Craig Stecyk, a rat skull in the spirit of a "pirate flag," becomes the logo of a new wheel: Rat Bones. Brad Bowman, Mike Folmer, Dave Andrecht and Bert Lamar go pro for Sims. The best skaters riding for Santa Cruz are still Duane Peters and the Alba brothers.

For a few more years yet, the bowl is the dominant terrain. Contests continue to take place, even during the slowest years, at the best parks in California, Marina del Rey (Santa Monica), Skate City (Whittier), The Ranch (Colton), Lakewood (Lakewood), Big O (Orange) and Pipeline (Upland). Duane Peters, Eddie Elguera and the young Steve Caballero vie for first place.

A group of money-less skaters try to sneak into Skate City in Whittier. The manager catches them and throws them out. John Lucero (a skater who rides for Varilfex), Richard Armejo and the rest of the group go to the parking lot and, hoping to provoke the manager, begin to skate the sidewalks and curbs as if they were the copping of bowls; they do "grinds," "rockslides" and even "inverts." The next day, Lucero and Armejo come back. The number of skaters who desert Skate City and join them grows daily. This is the beginning of *streetstyle*, the rebirth of street skating.

Steve Rocco and Rodney Mullen continue to invent more and more complex freestyle tricks. Mullen takes Alan Gelfand's trick, the "ollie," and starts doing it on the ground, which becomes the "flat ground ollie" (he unveils it during the Rusty Harris contest in Whittier that same year). It is the basis of an incalculable number of tricks to come. Under the name the "ollie prop pop," Rodney Mullen's trick is reproduced in Thrasher magazine, in a photo sequence entitled *Trick Tip*. Progressively, other skaters (such as Mark Gonzales, Natas Kaupas and Tommy Guerrero) would use it on the street and completely revolutionize *streetstyle* skating (soon abbreviated to "street"). The "ollie" would allow for the invention of new challenges, to ollie over benches and stairs, onto the highest ledges and handrails, where street skaters would transpose *lip-tricks* from vertical terrains.

1982

Powell Peralta brings out Tony Hawk's first pro-model. The Bones Brigade wins all the contests. Over the course of a single year, the company triples its sales. Billy Ruff skates for Gordon & Smith and is one of the best *vert-skaters* of the time. A new generation of skaters go pro this year: Mark Rogowski (Gordon & Smith), Lester Kasaï (Sims), Chris Miller (Gordon & Smith), Christian Hosoï (Sims), Lance Mountain (Variflex) and Neil Blender (Gordon & Smith).

Rodney Mullen invents three important variations of the "ollie": the "ollie kick flip," the "ollie heel flip" and (of lesser importance) the "ollie impossible." The first two consist of ollieing into the air while making the board spin once by kicking it with the front of your foot ("kick flip") or the heel ("heel flip") along a longitudinal axis. The Impossible consists of an "ollie" in which the board is vertically rotating 360° around the back foot before landing.

The concrete skatepark crisis extends to even the most famous parks. Cherry Hill was razed in 1981, and Lakewood and Big O come to share the same fate this year. The era of skateparks would not have lasted more than five years, from 1977 to 1982. Skateboarding goes back to the streets while modern wooden ramps find their form (they would, in turn, dominate skateboarding from 1984 to 1989).

The first Eurocana, a sort of international, informal skateboarding course is organized in Sweden. It features a handful of Bones Brigade skaters: Stacy Peralta, Alan Gelfand, Steve Caballero and Mike McGill. This is where American skaters discover the prototype of the modern ramp: a *half-pipe* with an expanse of flatness between two decks which feature steel coping. Ramp skating becomes a much more technical form than bowl skating, focusing more on tricks than on speed (skaters no longer do "lines" on ramps as they once did in bowls, but rather just go back and forth; the flat ground between transitions allows skaters find their footing after each trick).

It's on a ramp of this kind that the German company Titus Skate organizes the first Münster contest, which in the beginning is reserved exclusively for Europeans. The German Claus Grabke wins the first year.

Births of Chris Cole and Tony Trujillo.

1983

In Florida, Paul Schmitt dedicates himself to the full-time production of decks and creates Schmitt Stix. Monty Nolder is the first pro skater on the team. Variflex brings out Allen Losi's pro-model; John Lucero's is still in the process of being made. As for

Lance Mountain, he leaves Variflex and joins the Bones Brigade. To the detriment of its quality, Variflex begins marketing itself in the '80s toward large department stores. Christian Hosoï leaves Sims for Alva, which is slowly making a comeback. Tom Sims' company is in bad shape when Brad Dorfman offers to help him out while at the same time founding Vision Skateboards. After freestyler Don Brown's model comes out, Vision brings out Tom Groholski's *vert-rider*. Under the name of Vision Street Wear, Brad Dorfman is the first entrepreneur to associate his company with a line of skatewear (shoes and clothes).

Skate City, the famous park in Whittier (California), which was considered one of the few survivors of its kind, is razed. Around this time, the ramp gains popularity; more and more of them are built thanks to instructions published in rapidly sold copies of Thrasher magazine.

Mark Gonzales and Natas Kaupas are breaking ground in the street with new tricks. Their "ollies" attain impressive heights. They begin to ollie over stairs and gaps of all kinds. Street skating becomes a cross between *vert* and freestyle; Rodney Mullen's tricks which are based on "flips" are adapted to street skating at the same time that street skaters learn to ride on walls, taking off directly from the sidewalk without the help of any transition. The most important of the numerous tricks invented by Rodney Mullen this year is the "360 kickflip," an ollie which combines two kinds of rotation, a "360 degree pop-shovit" (where the board does a complete spin horizontal to the ground) and a kickflip.

The first street contest takes place in San Francisco's Golden Gate Park; first place goes to Tommy Guerrero, a young local, who is unknown at the time. Stacy Peralta immediately signs him on to the Bones Brigade. The trio of Tommy Guerrero, Mark Gonzales and Natas Kaupas would symbolize the supremacy of the three most important companies of the '80s: respectively, Powell Peralta, Vision and NHS (which owns Santa Cruz, Santa Monica Airlines, and, from 1986 on, Hosoï Skateboards).

Thanks to the initiative of Larry Balma (the founder of Tracker Trucks) and the United Skate Front (which consists of Peggy Cozens, Neil Blender, John Webster, Bryan Ridgeway, Garry

Scott Davis, Per Holknet, Grant Brittain and Balma himself) the first issue of Transworld magazine comes out in May, offering an alternative to the punk style of Thrasher. Transworld is conceived as an attempt to give skateboarding a better image. Peggy Cozens' article "Skate and Create" is a response to Craig Stecyk's article "Skate and Destroy," published in the first issue of Thrasher. The rivalry between the two magazines is heightened by the fact that the two main truck companies respectively own them: Fausto Vitello and Independent on one side, and Larry Balma and Tracker on the other.

In the United States, Steve Caballero and the rest of the Bones Brigade win almost all the contests throughout the year. Rodney Mullen loses the only contest of his entire career at Del Mar Skate Ranch to the Swede Per Welinder, who is invited to join the Bones Brigade. The first French championships of this new wave of skateboarding are organized in Rouen from the 1st to the 3rd of July.

1984

Mike McGill invents one of the most legendary tricks in the history of skateboarding on the Eurocana ramp in Sweden. This consists of an aerial composed of a semi flip combined with a 540 degree rotation. McGill unveils his new trick at the time of the most important contests of the year at Del Mar Skate Ranch (California). After him, Tony Hawk would be the first skater to pull off a "McTwist," followed by Lester Kasai, Christian Hosoï and Jeff Philips.

Christian Hosoï and Tony Hawk start battling for first place in various contests. They would soon be the two idols of the '80s, symbolizing, like Blackhart and Valdez before them (1978), style versus technique: an already classic dichotomy incarnated by the rivalry between Thrasher and Transworld, Santa Cruz and Powell Peralta, and Independent and Tracker.

After an initial attempt made in 1981 (a 16-minute video that was never really distributed), Powell Peralta brings out The Bones Brigade Video Show. Directed by Stacy Peralta and Craig Stecyk with a $15,000 budget, this is the first real skate video and becomes the model for all those to follow. The video, in the form of a VHS, would quickly sell 30,000 copies. In both individual and group sequences, the video shows the entire extent of the Bones Brigade, amateurs and pros alike, such as Steve Caballero, Adrian Demain, Todd Hastings, Tony Hawk, Chris Iverson, Mike McGill, Lance Mountain, Rodney Mullen, Stacy Peralta, Eddie Reategui, Kevin Staab, Steve Steadham and Per Welinder. The sound track from The Bones Brigade Video Show is created especially for the video (one of the characteristics of Powell Peralta videos); it features several groups, one of which is Steve Cabellero's The Faction, whose song "Skate and Destroy" opens the video.

Skaters have assimilated the punk aesthetic and their DIY credo. The hardcore punk groups composed of skaters create a rock genre known as skate rock: JFA, Agent Orange, The Faction, Aggression, McRad and The Suicidal Tendencies being the most famous. Music plays a significant role in skate culture; companies such as Rip City, Skull Skate and later Zorlac bring out decks named after bands like Black Flag, The Vandals, Gang Green and then Social Distortion, The Red Hot Chili Peppers and Metallica. The Suicidal Tendencies and JFA would even have their own skateboard companies.

Birth of Paul Rodriguez.

1985

Skateboarding more or less regains the same popularity it enjoyed at the end of the '70s. Brad Dorfman creates a business partnership with Paul Schmitt, providing him with a 4,500 square meter (50,000 square feet) factory. This is where 50,000 Vision, Sims and Schmitt Stix decks are produced every month. Vision brings out Mark Gonzales' first pro-model which, unsurprisingly, becomes its best seller. In 1978, a few years after the dissolution of Team Zephyr, Skip Engblom had created Santa Monica Airlines, a small company also known under the name SMA. At the end of the '70s, Jack Waterman left Sims to become the first pro skater for SMA. A few down years followed. But with age, Engblom hasn't lost his nose for good skating. He noticed Natas Kaupas, a young Santa Monica skater, and doesn't wait long to bring out his pro-model. Natas is Skip Engblom's only pro skater, but this hardly matters, because he is incredibly talented and deserves a team all to himself. Kevin Ancell creates the graphics for Natas' first deck. He associates him with a black panther, an image, which in the hands of different artists (Wes Humpston, Jim Phillips, Justin Forbes and Jimbo Phillips) would represent Natas until 1991.

Following the Swedish model, the Bourges' skate club (Les Berrichons Associés) organizes the first skate camp in France. Three Powell Peralta skaters are invited for the occasion: Per Welinder, Kevin Staab and Mike McGill. Grant Brittain, a <u>Transworld</u> photographer, is traveling through France. He would publish an article with images of the Berrichons Associés skate camp in the famous American magazine.

Sweden is decidedly a fertile ground for invention. Again, on the Eurocana ramp, Tony Hawk pulls off the first "720" (two consecutive and complete rotations in the air) as well as two other aerials, the "stale fish" (with his back hand, Hawk grabs his board mid air just behind his left foot) and the "one foot lien to tail" (the front hand grabs the nose, the front foot comes off the board, the back foot stays on the tail which hits against the coping before going back into the transition) renamed the "Madonna" by virtue of her popularity, which dates to the same year. Christian Hosoï himself invents the "rocket air" (an aerial during which he holds his deck by the nose while putting both his feet on the tail) and the "Christ air" (where he takes his feet entirely off the board and holds it in one hand with his arms spread out like Christ on the cross).

Powell Peralta's second video, <u>Future Primitive</u>, hits the market. Twice as long as the <u>Bones Brigade Video Show</u>, this new production by the duo Peralta/Stecyk shows every aspect of contemporary skateboarding. <u>Future Primitive</u> features: Steve Caballero, Adrian Demain, Richie Dunlap, Tommy Guerrero, Kevin Harris, Tony Hawk, Chris Iverson, Mike McGill, Lance Mountain, Rodney Mullen, Eric Sanderson, Steve Steadham, Ray Underhill and Per Welinder.

Robert Zemeckis' <u>Back to the Future</u> is a box-office hit. Michael J. Fox (Marty McFly) appears in the very first scenes with a Schmitt Stix skateboard under his arm. Catapulted 30 years into the past by accident (an experiment with his friend Doc goes awry), the young McFly finds himself in the year 1955 where, in order to escape a gang of bullies (who end up under a pile of manure), he invents the skateboard by tearing off the box on some kid's DIY scooter skate. Per Welinder is Michael J. Fox's stuntman.

1986
Vision brings out Mark "Gator" Rogowski's (who left Gordon & Smith) pro-model, one of the most visually memorable decks in the history of skateboarding: a kind of kinetic play of triangles which spiral into one another created, by Greg Evans. After doing Mark Gonzales' graphics, Andy Takakjian designs another hit, the Vision Psycho Stix; millions of skaters from all over the world remember this board by virtue of having appeared on the Australian band INXS' record cover for the album <u>Kick</u> in 1987.

On a Brooklyn rooftop, Rodney King, Bruno Musso and Aly Moore cut Shut Skateboards' first decks with a jigsaw. This impromptu wood shop then sets up shop in King's garage where they produce more than 4,000 decks in one year, 400 of which are painted with stencils and spray paint. Shut is the first New York skateboard company. Aside from Bruno Musso and Rodney Kind, Shut's team consists of a whole new generation of East Coast street skaters: Sean Sheffey, Chris "Dune" Pastras, Felix Arguelles, Rick Ibaseta, Coco Santiago, and Jeff Pang.

After a short stint with Powell Peralta and Madrid, the German Claus Grabke joins Santa Cruz. A number of European pros ride for American companies: the Swedes Per Welinder and Tony Magnusson skate respectively for Gordon & Smith and Uncle Wiggly's, Nicky Guerrero (Denmark) for Gordon & Smith, Don Brown (England) for Vision and Pierre-André Sénizergues (France) for Sims.

Schmitt Stix is the company on the rise; Paul Schmitt brings out three new pro-models: Joe Lopes, Jeff Grosso and John Lucero. George Yohn names his shoe company, which makes shoes expressly for skating, after a trick invented by Tony Hawk, Airwalk. The first skaters on the team (three *vert* riders) are Tony Magnusson, Lester Kasai and Tony Hawk.

Del Mar Skate Ranch, the concrete skate park in San Diego, has been closed for a few months, when the making of a B movie

(Thrashin') opens it again for a weekend. A number of professional skaters are hired as doubles or even actors, which allows Tony Hawk, Lester Kasaï, Kevin Staab, Christian Hosoï and a number of other skaters to ride Del Mar one last time. Thrashin' comes out in the United States at the end of the year. In France it would only be accessible in video stores under the name Skate Gang. The film recounts the story of a nice skater (played by Josh Brolin) who must prove himself against a gang of bad skaters in order to win the heart of a "beautiful" blond. On the movie poster, Brolin wears his wrist-guards backwards, a detail noticed by skaters everywhere. Bulldozers take care of Del Mar Skate Ranch the following year.

The ramp has definitively replaced the bowl as the dominant terrain. With "backside airs" 3.2 meters (10.4 feet) above coping, Christian Hosoï takes the world record for highest air. Steve Caballero officially beats this record the following year with a height of 3.35 meters (10.9 feet).

In parking lots, schoolyards and streets, jump ramps or street ramps are the rage. In San Francisco, skaters already begin to gather at Justin Herman Plaza. Conceived in 1971 by the architect Lawrence Halprin, this plaza, which is better known as the Embarcadero or even EMB, is part of the Golden Gateway, a project by SOM, a group of urbanists who work in the offices of Skidmore, Owings and Merill. The EMB is composed of a variety of structures, including a fountain. An enormous gap, which separates a wave-like concrete fortification from another concrete plane, is named the Gonz Gap, due to the fact that Mark Gonzales was the first to ollie it. Along with Natas Kaupas, Eric Dressen and the lesser-known Johnee Kop, Mark Gonzales shares the authorship of the first boardslides down handrails.

A 16-year-old skater from New Jersey named Mike Vallely takes first place in amateur ranking at the Oceanside street contest in Los Angeles. He is immediately spotted by Stacy Peralta and would quickly go on to become one of the new icons of street skating.

Germany's annual contest, held in Münster, becomes a European cup and opens this year to include street skating. The reputation of the Bourges skate camp grows. The second season hosts Tony Hawk and Kevin Staab.

1987

Powell Peralta launches a new ad campaign in magazines with the slogan: "Skateboarding is Not a Crime."

In order to meet the growing demands of his market, Skip Engblom joins forces with NHS. NHS houses SMA, Santa Cruz and Hosoï Skateboards, Christian Hosoï's company. The 27-year-old Steve Rocco, who has nothing aside from his reputation as an innovative skater, is kicked off team Sims by Brad Dorfman. Skip Engblom takes him under his wing and offers to start his own company under the aegis of SMA. Rocco joins up with John Lucero, who has just left Schmitt Stix. Rather than create a single company, the two found Prime Time, which houses their respective companies, on one side SMA Rocco Division, and on the other, Lucero Skateboards. But due to personal differences, John Lucero soon sells his part of the company to Rodney Mullen, who becomes Steve Rocco's new business partner, while continuing to skate professionally for Powell Peralta. Steve Rocco takes to being a businessman and is a fast learner. His first tactic consists of doubling the percentage pro-skaters earn on each deck their model sells (i.e., two dollars per deck instead of one). He thus succeeds in convincing Jessie Martinez to leave Vision and become the first pro-skater for SMA Rocco Division. This is a major development in the industry of skateboarding. Skaters begin to reflect on the royalty system, concluding that, if a small company is capable of offering two dollars a board, this means that the large companies are exploiting them.

For the end of Powell Peralta's third video, <u>The Search for Animal Chin</u>, Stacy Peralta asks Tim Payne to build a ramp without precedent. What he produces is no longer strictly speaking a ramp, but rather a complex of ramps built in the boonies, a desert landscape in Oceanside, California. From that moment on, Tim Payne becomes known as the most inventive ramp builder. The filming of <u>The Search for Animal Chin</u> lasts four months and concentrates on the five most popular skaters of the Bones Brigade: Steve Caballero, Mike McGill, Tony Hawk, Lance Mountain and Tommy Guerrero. Rodney Mullen, Kevin Harris and Per Welinder, the team's freestyle skaters, are barely even shown. The film is organized around an intrigue that is almost as well organized as an X film. A famous skater, the old Animal Chin, has disappeared, and with him, "the spirit of skateboarding." The Bones Brigade goes looking for him, and in doing so, end up skating the most famous spots of the time, from Wallos, the Hawaiian ditch, to the streets of San Francisco. The video comes out at the end of the year and skaters go crazy for it. It becomes a classic of the genre.

Jason Jesse, a professional vert-skater who rides for Santa Cruz and who is known for his Harley and his tattoos, invents the "pivot to fakie"; tricks which involve changing direction at the last moment ("revert") and going back into transition backwards ("fakie") become very popular. Chris Miller pulls off the first "backside lipslides" on vert; a trick which is extremely difficult, but which for the untrained eye might seem very simple: after a "backside 180 ollie" (a sort of half turn upon coming off the ramp) the skater slides backward along the coping with the bottom of his board, before re-entering the ramp.

The annual Münster contest in Germany becomes a world cup. The results of vert and street are absolutely identical: Steve Caballero takes first place, while Lance Mountain and Nicky Guerrero respectively take second and third. The French freestyle skater Jean-Marc Vaissette takes advantage of the absence of some of the biggest names in freestyle and wins. The contest also features slalom and roller skating.

The reputation of the ramp of Berrichons Associés and their skate camp is thoroughly established. After Münster, many skaters make a detour to Bourges (Chris Miller, Tony Hawk, Mark Gonzales, Kevin Staab, Joe Johnson, Christian Hosoï, and Mark "Gator" Rogowski).

In the tradition of The Faction's "Skate and Destroy," The Suicidal Tendencies, Mike Muir's band (whose brother is Jim Muir, the ex-Team Zephyr rider and co-founder of Dogtown Skateboards) yells "Possessed To Skate." The song is from the album <u>Join The Army</u>, which comes out this year:

Let's skate!
Seemed like such an innocent toy
He was the All-American boy

Got a skate at eight years old
Now the story can be told

Beware he's possessed to skate!

Skating takes him up in height
He's a pilot on a modern flight
See him flying through the air
If he don't land then he don't care

Cause he rips-he rips
When he skates-he skates
Cause he never hesitates
[…]

1988

According to Time Magazine, there are an estimated twenty million skaters in the U.S.

The form of the skateboard deck is still quite uncertain; it varies quite a bit from board to board.
    Dogtown and Alva are back on top as popular companies. A magazine ad shows the entire Alva team posing in a small street in Chicago; they are dressed in jeans and leather with long hair and dreads, with the exception of one shaved head, which belongs to Bill Danforth.
    Schmitt Stix brings out Chris Miller's pro-model with a long, upturned nose (around 12 cm, 4.2 inches). Until that time, the nose of boards was almost flat and rarely longer than 5 cm (2 inches). Lighter and more maneuverable, Freetsyle decks are thin, perfectly symmetrical (the tail and the nose have the same length and the sides are straight) and are without concave. Freestylers ride them in either sense, meaning there is no front or back.
    Tony Magnusson is a Swedish vert-rider who immigrated to the United States. With the help of Mike Ternasky, he founds H-Street. Tired of waiting for Powell Peralta to turn him pro, Danny Way, the young prodigy of the Bones Brigade, leaves the most famous team at the time, and turns pro for H-Street. He barely makes it into their first video.

SMA Rocco Division decks are good sellers. Steve Rocco decides to start producing wheels as well. In an ad for Gizmo Wheels, he reveals that all skate wheels, no matter what company they come from, are the same, since all of them, without exception, come from the same factory. The directors of NHS, the official distributors of Santa Monica Airlines and the owners of the famous company Santa Cruz, are furious. Santa Cruz wheels, Speedwheels, are among the most popular on the market and represent an important percentage of their sales. Skip Engblom, who had originally invited Rocco to start his own company under the aegis of SMA, is forced by NHS to no longer allow Steve Rocco to use the SMA label. Meanwhile, Powell Peralta leads Rodney Mullen, who is Rocco's business partner but before anything a member of the Bones Brigade, to understand that it is not in his interest to continue working with the competition. The two companies seem to realize the potential danger posed by SMA Rocco Division and H-Street. Following the example of Danny Way, Rodney Mullen and Mike Vallely quit Powell Peralta. The two of them become partners with Steve Rocco and help him found World Industries.

Mullen and Vallely are both pro riders for the team and business partners; World Industries is the first company of the new generation run entirely by skaters. Thanks to the 30,000 dollars brought to the enterprise by the two ex-Bones Brigaders, World Industries manages to launch Mike Vallely's pro-model toward the end of the year. Vallely's model is the first double-tail (which is to say, the tail and the nose are identical). In order to produce this kind of deck, Rocco makes a deal with a technician who had just made a mould of the same kind for Vision, which should have the exclusive rights to the mould, but like Rocco, the technician in question has a bone to pick with his employer, Brad Dorfman (the same Brad Dorfman who had kicked Rocco out of Sims in 1987). Mike Vallely's pro model, known as the Mike Vallely Animal Farm, would come out at the beginning of 1989.

Public Domain, Powell Peralta's fourth video, is much more comprehensive than its previous production. The entire Bones Brigade is in it, which is to say, 28 skaters, both professional and amateurs alike. A whole new generation of vert-riders is discovered (Danny Way, Bucky Lasek, and Colin McKay...) as well as a large number of street skaters (Jim Thiebaud, Mike Vallely, Ray Barbee, Frankie Hill, and Chet Thomas...).

By foregoing a professional cameraman, H-Street revolutionizes the aesthetic of skate videos. For <u>Shackle Me Not</u>, Tony Magnusson and Mike Ternasky simply hand over the video cameras and let the skaters film each other whenever they feel like it.

Contrary to <u>Public Doman,</u> <u>Shackle Me Not</u> is shot and produced with the worst quality filming. Nevertheless, the "Do It Yourself" aesthetic legacy so dear to punk music still manages to seduce young skaters.

While <u>Public Doman</u> and <u>Shackle Me Not</u> both feature some odd thirty skaters in each video, for its first video, <u>Wheels of Fire</u>, Santa Cruz decides to limit itself to six skaters: Steve Alba, Claus Grabke, Christian Hosoï, Natas Kaupas, Jeff Kendall and Rob Roskopp who cover, between the six of them, every possible form of skateboarding, from concrete skateparks to street, ramps and downhill skating. Hosoï and Natas Kaupas' parts are both legendary. The soundtrack includes bands such as Black Flag, Sonic Youth, The Descendents, and Firehose. It opens with a memorable song by Claus Grabke's band, Eight Dayz. Very rock'n'roll, <u>Wheels of Fire</u> confirms NHS's reputation.

From now on, the skate video is the primary promotional tool for skateboard companies. It is through this medium that they create their identities. Homes begin to be equipped with VHS players Thus videos help young skaters to analyze, digest and comprehend the tricks performed by professionals much more easily. In this way, watching videos significantly accelerates the evolution of a skater's skill.

Symbolically, they start to replace contest results. The "Peralta method" which consists of waiting for a skater to do well in contests before going pro has become antiquated. The best skaters are no longer just those who win the most competitions, but also those who have the best video parts. Despite never being prizewinners, Natas Kaupas and Mark Gonzales are two important examples of skaters who have had a massive impact upon skateboarding.

Outside of the usual circuits of video making, the surfer and "chief operator" Mike McEntire produces at his own expense and in a VHS edition of 1000 copies, Sick Boys. Filmed with a Super 8 camera and fisheye lens over the course of 1987, Sick Boys documents the emergence of street skating in San Francisco. The film brings together the best street skaters of the time and place: Tommy Guerrero, Mic-E Reyes, Natas Kaupas, Julian Stranger, Jim Thiebaud and Ron Allen.

Pipeline, the last of the "great" concrete skateparks, is closed to the public. It would be destroyed in April of 1989.

Skaters begin to build mini-ramps: ramps without vert whose height is between 1.5 (5 feet) and 2.6 meters (8.5 feet). This form of skating, half way between vert and street, contributes to bringing new tricks to vert skating by borrowing them from street skating.

In Vancouver, Kevin Harris, a Canadian freestyler who rides for the Bones Brigade, has his own skatepark built: a complex of wooden ramps and bowls of shapes and sizes that transcends the mastery of Tim Payne; this is where one of the first mini-ramp contests takes place.

At the end of March, the Eiffel Tour's ponds are empty and clean again. The sessions are renewed and the spot becomes legendary. During the summer, many American pro-skaters come to skate it: Steve Caballero, Lester Kasai, Natas Kaupas, and Mark Gonzales. It is a historic summer for skateboarding in Paris. The ponds are filled up again the first weekend of October. In Streets on Fire, the second Santa Cruz video that comes out in 1989, Claus Grabke and Jeff Hedges skate the former spot.

Street skaters continue to appropriate Rodney Mullen's tricks. Jason Lee and Ed Templeton pull off 360 kickflips and ollie impossibles, Matt Hensley does backside 180 kickflips (a backside half turn in the air during which the board flips once underneath the feet). Ed Templeton, Natas Kaupas and Mark Gonzales start "grinding" handrails, which is to say, ollieing onto and going down a handrail balanced on their trucks.

In Münster, Christian Hosoï takes first place in vert. In street, first place goes to Steve Caballero for the second year in a row. Beating Tony Hawk, Hosoï wins another equally important contest organized by Vision Skateboards, the Vision Skate Escape. For the occasion, Tim Payne constructs a vert ramp and a mini-ramp, which are linked by a spine (a double coping without platform). One of the platforms is transformed into a stage for a concert, which stars the Red Hot Chili Peppers, associated at the time with skate rock.

Nintendo brings out the first skateboarding video game: Skate or Die. Sega has another video game, California Games, which features in a single game skateboarding, surfing, roller skating, BMXing, frisbee throwing and hackysacking.

1989

Decks are about 78 cm (30 inches) long and 25 cm (10 inches) wide. Tails are much longer (15 cm, 6 inches) and more raised than the noses, which are rarely longer than 10 cm (4 inches). A complete skateboard weighs around 1.5 kg (3.3 lbs). The standard diameter of a wheel is 65 mm (2.46 inches). Street wheels are not as large, between 57 (2.24 inches) and 61 mm (2.4 inches) and not as hard, while freestyle wheels are even harder and smaller. Even though new companies like Toxic and Cockroach enter the market, Bones wheels (Powell Peralta) and Speedwheels (Santa Cruz) are the most popular. World Industries brings out Mike Vallely's pro-model, an unprecedented board: the first double tail, or 'double-kick' as it became known. The nose and the tail have the same form, while the latter is a little bit longer. For the board, Marc Mckee creates a graphic that is totally opposed to the trend of skeletons and monsters. Colorful and faux-naïf, Mike Vallely's animal farm is closer to Walt Disney cartoons than to Marvel comics. Other World Industries decks, as well as the second Vallely pro-model, are more traditional: the nose is long, but more narrow than the tail. A few months later, Vision also brings out a double tail (two actually, one that is a standard size, and another that is a bit smaller). But the fame of Mike Vallely, whom many consider to be the best street skater at the time, as well as what gives World Industries its cutting edge, leaves Vision in the dust. Vision's prospects grow worse when Mark Gonzales, their main street skater, decide to team up with Steve Rocco in order to found his own company, which he ironically names Blind. This makes it clear that he is situating himself very much against

Vision. Jason Lee leaves World Industries and joins Blind; Guy Mariano and Rudy Johnson (two new fugitives from the Bones Brigade), Jordan Richter and Danny Way (who quits H-Street in 1990 and goes straight to Blind) would all soon follow him. Paul Schmitt splits with Brad Dorfman (Vision and Sims). He sets up shop in a little factory known as PS Stick and concentrates on making his own boards.

The inventor of the "feeble grind" (a variation of grinding), Tod Swank is both a photographer and long time collaborator with Transworld magazine. Encouraged by Steve Rocco, he sells his Harley for $5,000 and starts his own company, Foundation Skateboards.

Tim Puimarta, an engineer who works for Santa Cruz, experiments with *everslick*, a thin layer of thermoplastic glued to the bottom of the board. *Everslick*, a little like the plastic rails which it helps render obsolete, produces a board that can slide on any surface. This innovation also allows for photographic prints on the bottom of boards, which would briefly give skateboard graphics a new lease on life. Before disappearing completely in 1993, the Everslick would be produced by every company between 1990 and 1992.

When Pierre-André Sénizergues begins his career as a professional freestyler in the United States, he takes advantage of the situation and rents a small space and begins distributing Etnics, made by a small French shoe company. Due to a legal problem, Etnics changes a single letter and becomes Etnies. The company just barely survives and Sénizergues ends up buying it. After Vans, Airwalk and Vision Street Wear, Etnies becomes the fourth skate shoe company. This year, Pierre-André Sénizergues launches the first signature shoe (which is to say, a shoe named after a skater) the Natas Kaupas.

Vans, which, thanks to the help of an investor, barely avoids bankruptcy, brings out shoes named after Steve Caballero. The success is immediate. Otherwise, it would be five years before any other skaters would have their own signature shoes.

Absorbed by street skating, freestyle is a dying mode of skateboarding. In Rubbish Heap, the first World Industries video, which comes out this year, Jeremy Klein "focuses" (i.e., breaks) Rodney Mullen's board, thereby forcing him to skate a street board. Rodney Mullen's last freestyle model comes out in 1990. Afterward, freestyle boards will no longer be made.

Danny Way begins introducing street tricks into ramp skating. This year, he pulls off the first "Indy kickflip," an aerial that consists of lightly kicking the board so that it flips and is caught by the back hand just before re-entering transition. Like the "McTwist" from a few years before, the "Indy kickflip" indicates a turning point in the evolution of ramp tricks.

Skateboarding is banned on the sidewalks of Venice Beach. In response to a new wave of laws against skateboarding, Powell Peralta's new video is entitled Ban This. In the form of a mythical sticker, the slogan "Skateboarding is not a crime" invades streets and boards everywhere. Ban This (Powell Peralta), Hokus Pokus (H-Street) and Streets on Fire (Santa Cruz) take up where Public Domain, Shackle me not, and Wheels of Fire left off. Santa Cruz picks up some excellent new skaters such as Tom Knox and Eric Dressen. Street skating is even more present; in Rubbish Heap (World Industries), it dominates every other kind of form.

A skatepark, straight from the '70s (concrete no coping) is built in a part of downtown Montpellier (France) known as Antigone. But the local residents and shop owners immediately start complaining about the noise and acts of vandalism that accompany the skaters. Even though the park would be razed and covered with dirt in 1991, it would still find the time to host several contests as well as demo by Team Santa Cruz during their European tour. A nice patch of green grass covers the site of the park today.

In an Ollie Contest in Hawaii, Matt Hensley manages to get up to 84 cm (33 inches). Tony Hawk and Lance Mountain respectively win the ramp skating and street skating contests in Münster.

In June, while the first issue of Noway, a magazine exclusively dedicated to skateboarding, comes out in France, Thrasher celebrates its 100th issue. A chronology retraces in six pages the nine years of its existence. A history of skate decks, as well as interviews with Duane Peters, Steve Caballero, Tony Hawk and Christian Hosoï complete this special issue, which has contributed to the establishment of this chronology of skateboarding.

The Simpsons, created by Matt Groening, enters its first season. In record time, long before Tony Hawk, Bart Simpson becomes the most famous skater on the planet.

The American artist Dan Graham conceives a maquette for his Skateboard Pavilion, an architectural project that contains a concrete bowl covered by a pyramidal glass roofing entirely constituted by mirrors without tin. What is more, to paraphrase Graham speaking of the piece himself, the work encourages graffiti on a piece of "public" sculpture. The Skateboard Pavilion would never be built.

Birth of Ryan Sheckler.

1990

More and more skaters are leaving big companies to start or join smaller teams. It is the end of the hegemony of the grand trio from the '80s: Vision/Powell Peralta/Santa Cruz. Brad Dorfman is the first to feel the effects. After the departure of Mark Gonzales and the arrest for murder of Mark "Gator" Rogowski, Vision no longer has a single power skater. Powell Peralta and Santa Cruz are still in the running, but young skaters are beginning more and more to buy from smaller companies.

Skateboarding, its industry and its influences have changed. Paul Schmitt decides to start over again from zero. He buries Schmitt Stix and launches New Deal. Named artistic director, the skater Andy Howell is one of the first people to base a visual identity of a skate company on hip-hop culture. Like Rocco, Paul Schmitt and Andy Howell innovate in terms of commercial strategy. They begin by distributing a promotional video before New Deal products hit the skate shops. Justin Girard, Ed Templeton, Tim Brauch, Armando Barajas and Ron Knigge are some of the excellent new skaters who ride for New Deal. Success is immediate. Powell Peralta and SMA lose two more skaters. Tommy Guerrero and Jim Thiebaud found Real under the umbrella of Deluxe, Fausto Vitello's distribution company (Independent, Thunder, Spitfire). A partner of the new company, Jeff Klindt designs the Real logo as well as the graphics for Tommy Guerrero's new pro-model. While John Lucero starts up Black Label, H-Street becomes the distributor of Planet Earth, Chris Miller's company.

Together, Neil Blender, Chris Carter and Mike Hill found Alien Workshop.

H-Street skaters are known for doing handrails. Sal Barbier is the first skater to pull off a kickflip boardslide.

On the same five stairs handrail, Jason Carney pulls off a backside lipslide. These tricks are documented in <u>This is not the New H-Street Video</u> (1991), but a little too late. Santa Cruz brings out <u>Speed Freaks</u>, a video which features skaters who ride for Speed Wheels.

Accompanied by "Freak Scene," by Dinosaur Jr., Mike Vallely can be seen on his double kick skateboard. Although a bit drawn out (31 skaters in 72 minutes), the scenes with Vallely, Danny Way, Christian Hosoï, Natas Kaupas and Tom Knox make it a classic.

In two years, Powell Peralta has lost many skaters, but this is not what renders their new video <u>Propaganda</u> problematic. Stacy Peralta seems to be hesitating between two eras and two tendencies: remaining faithful to his aesthetic and the oldest riders of the Bones Brigade, or opening up the field to a new generation of street skaters such as Lance Conklin, Chet Thomas, Salman Agah, Frank Hirata and Ray Barbee. Too quickly forgotten at the beginning of the '90s by exclusively technical skaters, Frankie Hill's part is one of the most memorable. His final "gap," an ollie over a small landscape that separates two levels of a parking lot, prefigures a style of skating that would emerge at the end of the '90s with skaters such as Jamie Thomas, Chad Muska and Heath Kirchart.

Jason Lee and some of his friends appear in Sonic Youth's video for <u>100%</u> directed by Spike Jonze.

In Portland, Oregon, on the parking lot of an abandoned hotel situated under the Burnside bridge, Mark Hubbard and Mark Scott begin to build a concrete skatepark without any authorization. A neighboring construction site gives them sacks of cement for nothing. A permanent work in progress, Burnside evolves as the interests and needs of skaters progress, and each year new layers of concrete are added to it. Later, under the names of Grindline and Dreamland, Hubbard and Scott would become officially renowned as two of the best designers of concrete skateparks.

Jean-Pierre Colinet, a final year architecture student in Marseille, France, designs and supervises the construction of a concrete skatepark that the municipality of Marseille decides to locate at Prado Beach. Situated on the waterfront, and not far from the city center, the Prado park is complete success. In Bourges, Les Berrichons Associés build a large, wooden bowl. Wooden skateparks are being built more and more frequently in France; the one in Blagnac (near Toulouse) is the most famous. Noway, the only specialized skate magazine in France, becomes Anyway. Akin to Thrasher, Anyway publishes how-to construction plans for modules and skate ramps.

A Santa Cruz skater, the Englishman Bod Boyle, beats Chris Miller and Danny Way, taking first place in vert at Münster; it's the first time that the Americans lose at Münster since the contest became a world cup. In street, however, first place goes to the new star of New Deal, Ed Templeton. A few days after Münster, the world cup of Le Grand-Bornand takes place in France. Templeton goes on to take first place there as well, while Chris Miller takes first place in vert. Thrasher reintroduces an old '70s tradition of naming a Skater of the Year. This year the trophy goes to Tony Hawk, a skater who is far from incarnating the punk spirit of the magazine.

1991

While new companies continue to start up, the market takes another downturn.

A huge loss for SMA, Natas Kaupas partners up with Steve Rocco and founds 101 (One O One), a division of World Industries whose empire continues to spread. Besides Natas, team 101 would soon be comprised of Gabriel Rodriguez, Kris Markovich, Adam McNatt, Leigh Peterson and Eric Koston.

Since there are just too many skaters who ride for H-Street, Tony Magnusson starts up a sub-division of the company called Life.

With the help of Steve Rocco, Mike Ternasky (formerly partnered with Tony Magnusson) decides to start his own company, Plan B. Matt Hensley, Mike Carroll, Sean Sheffey and Sal Barbier, who are four of the best H-Street skaters, decide to follow him. Colin McKay and Rick Howard leave Powell Peralta and Blockhead and join Plan B as well. Danny Way (for whom

Blind just brought out a pro-model) and Pat Duffy, a young amateur who is still unknown, complete the team. Rodney Mullen had wanted to take advantage of the obsolescence of freestyle in order to retire from skating and concentrate on the development of World Industries (which he co-owns with Steve Rocco), but Mike Ternasky convinces him to start skating street, and he becomes a Plan B pro.

While everyone's eyes seem to be on Steve Rocco, Mike Vallely leaves World Industries for New Deal. He participates in the shooting of 1281, New Deal's second video which comes out in 1992. His inconsistency when it comes to being sponsored would become notorious.

Stacy Peralta splits up with George Powell to devote himself to directing films. This is one of the most significant events of the end of this year and the symbol of the end of an era; from 1992 on, Powell Peralta becomes (or rather, goes back to) Powell.

Spike Jonze is in charge of shooting Video Days, Blind's first video. In 20 minutes, four skaters establish the basis of the *new school*, foreshadowing the family of tricks of the next ten years to come. Mark Gonzales and Guy Mariano start to skate in *switch* stance (they change their front footing, which is the equivalent of a right-handed person writing with the left). Mark Gonzales pulls off a boardslide on a long handrail with two kinks (flat areas), he ollies the Wallenberg steps and invents the "darkslide" (a boardslide on the top side of the board, which Rodney Mullen will go on to develop the following year). Jason Lee and Rudy Johnson are both skaters who have extremely fluid styles. They have perfectly mastered freestyle tricks and manage to adapt them to any and every obstacle. On a ledge, Jason Lee pulls off, for example, the first "kickflip backside tailslide" (after a kickflip and a 90 degree rotation, he slides backwards along the tail of his skateboard on the edge of a bank). The video would have been perfect if the untimely departure of Danny Way had not prevented him from contributing a part. Despite all his talent, Jordan Richer, the only vert skater featured in the video, could not compete with the dexterity of such skaters as Danny Way or Colin McKay.

In San Francisco, the Embarcadero becomes the daily meeting spot for hundreds of skaters; it is emblematic of the renaissance of street skating. Thanks to videos and magazines, skaters from all over the world know every nook and cranny of the place without ever having set foot in it. The various concrete constructions which compose EMB all have their own names: The Stage, The C-Block, The Wave, The Big Stage, The Medium Stage, The Seven, The Little Three, The Big Three, The Fountain Curb and, of course, the famous Gonz Gap.

Hubba Hideout is a ledge (a kind of concrete hand railing) located close to the Embarcadero. "Hubba" is slang for drugs, meaning that the spot is a place to buy drugs. Wade Speyer inaugurates this famous spot this year with a "nose grind" (a "grind" with the front truck on the ledge).

In Münster, while Danny Way tries to pull off the "900" (an "aerial" composed of two and half complete rotations), Tony Hawk takes first place in both street and ramp. Hawk also wins the final year of Le Grand-Bornand world cup in France. In street, first place goes to Omar Hassan. Danny Way is named Thrasher's *Skater of the Year*.

1992

A decline in sales affects the global market. This third skateboard crash however is not as brutal as the first two.

Boards are becoming longer and thinner. They are about 80 cm (31 inches) long and 20 cm (7.8 inches) wide. From the nose to the tail, the sides run parallel to one another, and are very far from the "fish" shapes of the '80s. Noses are now much longer and more upturned while the tails have shrunk. The thickness of the board layers is now getting thinner. Skateboards become lighter but also much more fragile. World Industries is suspected of deliberately making fragile skateboards so that skaters, whose number are diminishing, buy more boards. The diameter of wheels likewise diminishes, and wheels are no longer any larger than 44 mm (1.7 inches); the smallest going as far down as 38 mm (1.5 inches). They are also the hardest they have ever been since the use of urethane. The width of trucks has been adapted to the width of boards. So that the screws don't get damaged by curbs and ledges when doing "nose slides" and "tail slides" two new holes are drilled more toward the interior of the truck base. During the transition from the old to the new standard, the base plate of each truck and board has six holes drilled through them. Skaters thus choose the position that makes the most sense in terms of what they use and the tricks they do; this simple gesture is actually enough to let people know whether to classify you as old or new school.

All of these innovations tend to facilitate tricks that are based on kickflips and slides. Very technical, these tricks are most often done going very slowly and close to the ground. Obstacles have a tendency to become very low. Skateboarding loses its breadth; we are far from the Natas of <u>Streets on Fire</u> or the Frankie Hill of <u>Propaganda</u>.

This powerful style of skateboarding does not, however, disappear entirely. Skaters like Danny Way, Pat Duffy, Wade Speyer, John Cardiel, Kris Markovich and Jeremy Wray keep it alive while also modernizing it.

Hard, small wheels can only be used on extremely smooth surfaces. Skateboarding is no longer perceived the way it once was, skaters use their boards less and less as a simple vehicle of transportation, and skating from one spot to another is no longer considered to be a part of a given session. Skateboarding becomes sedentary; skaters remain longer in a given place than before. The discovery of new spots is no longer as important as it once was. Skaters concentrate on tricks that are more often than not pulled off individually (given their difficulty), and no longer among a series or a *line* of other tricks. Certain tricks from the '80s like "grabs" ("ollies" in which the skater catches the board with a hand), the "no comply" and the "boneless" (tricks which require putting one foot on the ground) are totally rejected by the *new school*. Those who do not conform to the protocols of this kind of skateboarding, to its tricks as well as quasi-hip hop fashion, (baggy pants, and XXL T-shirts) are marginalized.

New companies continue to start up. Tony Hawk and Per Welinder leave Powell and found Birdhouse. Jeremy Klein abandons World Industries only to rejoin them. Birdhouse also features Willy Santos and Steve Berra (Ocean Howell and Mike Frazier would not become Birdhouse riders until the following year). Ray Barbee follows Lance Mountain who inaugurates The Firm.

1992

Mike McGill, manager of his own skatepark, retires from professional skateboarding. As for Powell, the only remaining original member of the Bones Brigade is Steve Caballero. Consolidated is a company founded by Jason Jesse, an ex-Santa Cruz rider. Meanwhile, Andy Howell launches Underworld Element, a subdivision of New Deal, whose team is already saturated with riders; the company would soon be known as Element.

On the East Coast, financial problems and bad choices regarding questions of distribution bring on the end of Shut Skateboards. Over the course of the past two years, many Shut skaters had left the team to ride for Californian companies. Jason Lee, Chris "Dune" Pastras and Kareem Campbell quit Blind and World Industries to found Blue while a couple of ex-New Deal riders, Ed Templeton and Mike Vallely, start up TV; like many others (Life, Acme, Union, Color...), the existence of Blue and TV would be short lived.

The dominant shoe style is for low tops. New School skaters wear Adidas (Gazelle and Superstar models) and Pumas (Clyde model) that they prefer to skateboarding shoes. For about a year, skaters have been DIY redesigning their own high top Airwalk and Vision skate shoes beneath the ankle. Vis-à-vis with this phenomenon, Steve Caballero persuades Vans to bring out a low top version of his signature shoe. The success of the Half Cab is immediate.

Questionable, Plan B's first video becomes an instant classic. In addition to incredibly technical sessions in the tradition of Video Days, Pat Duffy and Danny Way do grinds and boardslides down enormous handrails. Colin McKay and Danny Way have a similar profile, they are both very multitalented skaters capable of being innovative in both ramp and street skating. They adapt their expansive repertoire of street tricks to ramp skating and in doing so, manage to contribute to the renaissance of this declining form; it would take other ramp-riders a few years before they even get to the same level. As in street skating, ramp skaters start learning how to skate "backwards," more commonly known as *switch-stance.* Questionnable is dedicated to Matt Hensley, who retires at a young age from professional skateboarding after his unforgettable parts in the H-Street videos. Before progressively slipping into oblivion, SMA brings out Freedom of Choice, its first independent skate video (before this, Skip Englom's skaters were always part of Santa Cruz videos) and introduces a handful of unorthodox skaters, such as Jason Adams, Tim Brauch, Israel Forbes and Ron Whaley. Just like the number of companies, skate videos proliferate: Love Child (World Industries), Tim and Henry's Pack of Lies (Blind), Feasters (Birdhouse), Memory Screen (Alien Workshop) The Firm (The Firm), Debby does Blockhead (Blockhead's last video), Chaos (Powell), Da Deal is Dead (New Deal), Next Generation (H-Street), The Acme Skateboard Video (Acme), Right to Skate (Union) all come out this year.

Gabriel Leuret, a sixty-year-old ex-Muscat producer, creates an unprecedented skatepark (based on a ski resort) in the south of France between Nîmes and Montpellier: at the Rooler Gab park, skaters can get to the top of a little mountain thanks to a lift and then speed down an asphalt run 1.6 km long (1 mile) whose every turn features a concrete bank.

Steve Rocco brings out a new skate magazine called Big Brother. The first issue of Slap also comes out this year; this is the only magazine that is not directly linked to a big name in the skateboarding industry. Thrasher bestows the title of *Skater of the Year* on John Cardiel, a multi-talented skater who rides for Black Label (John Lucero's company). For only one year, Münster becomes a European cup again. Rune Glifberg, from Denmark, takes first place in ramp while the German Sami Harithi wins street.

1993
In order to unite the different divisions of New Deal, Paul Schmitt, Steve Douglas and Andy Howell found Giant Distribution. Steve Douglas and Josh Friedberg also bring out the first video magazine: 411. Chris Ortiz is the artistic director, expertly supervising the filming as well as the editing and the sound tracks. 411 is bi-monthly. In New York, Rodney Smith partners with Eli Gesner and Adam Schatz to start up Zoo York. After the last H-Street video comes out (Lick), Tony Magnusson changes the name of his company, which becomes Evol, but it doesn't last long. Breaking with Kareem Campbell, Jason Lee and Chris Pastras found Stereo

in the place of Blue. Ed Templeton starts up Toy Machine without Mike Vallely's help.

Just as Virtual Reality, Plan B's second video, confirms the supremacy of the company, Rick Howard has a disagreement with Mike Ternasky. A tough blow for Steve Rocco, who saw himself as beyond this sort of problem, Rick Howard, Mike Caroll, Megan Baltimore and the director Spike Jonze found Girl Skateboards. Eric Koston, Rudy Johnson, Guy Mariano, Sean Sheffey, Tim Gavin, Tony Fergusson and Jovantae Turner all leave their respective sponsors (World Industries, Plan B, Blind and 101) and start riding for Girl. The first Girl video, Goldfish, directed by Spike Jonze, comes out at the end of the year. Like many videos after 1992, Goldfish consists exclusively of street skating.

Although he is the founder of Blind, Mark Gonzales leaves the company and starts riding for Real with his friends in San Francisco. At the Embarcadero, he is the first to do a kickflip over the gap, which is named after him (Gonz Gap). Kris Markovich pulls off the same trick over another legendary gap in Carlsbad. Markovich is also the founder of Color, an ephemeral company whose only video comes out this year.

The Americans return to Münster. Tony Hawk takes first place in ramp and second place in street behind Ed Templeton. Thrasher's title of *Skater of the Year* goes to Salman Agah, a new recruit of Real and one of the pioneers of switch-stance.

The first issue of the magazine Juice comes out in November. It features an interview with Tony Alva as well as two legendary bands, Bad Brains and the Ramones. In 1998, the magazine's subtitle *Sounds, Surf & Skate* would be replaced by *Pools, Pipes & Punk Rocks*. Juice would identify a new generation of older skaters and would become without a doubt the most serious skateboarding magazine.

1994

Blind and 101 are dying companies, and Steve Rocco's supremacy is rapidly nearing its end. The "coup de grâce" is provided when Rick Howard and Mike Caroll found Chocolate, a sub-division of Girl. A new handful of skaters leave World Industries to ride for Chocolate.

Ronnie Bertino, Pat Channita and Jeremy Wray team up with Pat Duffy, Rodney Mullen, Sal Barbier, Colin McKay and Danny Way for Plan B, who take advantage of such a great team to produce their third video: Second Hand Smoke. The video is successful (Jeremy Wray's part is particularly spectacular). But in spite of such success, it's clear that the best skaters of the moment ride for Girl. Very soon afterward, Mike Ternasky dies in a car accident. Plan B would never be the same. With his disappearance, the company vegetates; their fourth video wouldn't come out until 1997.

Andy Howell quits Giant in order to dedicate himself to a career as a painter and a graphic artist. Johnny Schilleref replaces him as artistic director. Justin Girard, an early New Deal skater, launches a wheel company under Giant: Golden State Wheel.

Ed Templeton and Tod Swank found Tum Yeto, a distribution company that brings together their respective enterprises, Toy Machine and Foundation.

In San Francisco, under the umbrella of Deluxe Distribution, Julian Stranger and John Cardiel start Antihero.

The Englishmen Tom Penny and Geoff Rowley as well as the Dane Rune Glifberg move to California. They all ride for Flip, an English company known until that time as Death Box. Initially composed uniquely of European skaters, Flip would soon destabilize the notion of American supremacy.

Under the aegis of Droors Clothing, Damon Way and Ken Block found DC shoes. With Duffs, Steve Rocco and Rodney Mullen plunge into the shoe industry while in Australia Globe shoes hits the market. Tony Magnusson, Brian Reid, Tony Chen and C.S. Chen create the distribution company Alias. They start Evol Footwear which two years later would be renamed Osiris.

Signature shoes proliferate. Tony Hawk and Jason Lee both have their own shoes with Airwalk; DC brings out models by Danny Way and Colin McKay; the Salman Agah is produced by Vans and the Sal Barbier by Etnies. As with their pro-model decks, skaters earn a percentage of the sales of their signature shoes.

Tony Hawk pulls off a "540 kickflip" (a 540 degree aerial mixed with a kickflip), thus proving his enduring ability to not only stay up to date but also help skateboarding evolve. Heath Kirchart does a "kickflip to frontside boardslide" down a 7 stairs handrail (which is to say, he slides down a handrail after having done an ollie kickflip to get onto it) while Jeremy Wray does a frontside 360 ollie over the Carlsbad gap.

In Münster, Mike Frazier takes first place in ramp while Ethan Fowler, a Toy Machine skater, beats Wade Speyer and Ed Templeton, taking first place in street.

The title of *Skater of the Year* goes to Mike Carroll, one of the best street skaters for Girl and one of the stars of the EMB.

After 36 issues, B-Side magazine comes to an end. France's next skate magazine won't see the light of day until 1997.

Following the example of influential hardcore punk bands, the photographer Glen E. Friedman creates his own publishing house, Burning Flag Editions, and brings out his first book of photography, Fuck you Heroes. The images in Fuck you Heroes, which cover a period from 1976 to 1991, document the birth of modern skateboarding (along with Craig Stecyk, Friedman was the "official" Dogtown photographer), hardcore punk and rap. Glen E. Friedman's photos have contributed to the establishment of this chronology of skateboarding.

Even though the trend for music in videos is hip-hop, the company Stereo innovates: every part of its first video, A Visual Sound, is accompanied by jazz. Meanwhile, other non-conformist skaters are known to hum the words to Pavement's "Range Life" as they skate:

    Out on my skateboard the night is just hummin
    And the gumsmacks are the pulse I'll follow
    If my walkman fades then I got
    Absolutely no one
    No one but myself to blame.

1995

A new wave of skateboarding prohibitions spreads across the United States. Skateboarding is forbidden at the Embarcadero, Love Park (i.e. JFK Plaza in Philadelphia), and Pulaski Park (Washington).

Wheels return to a normal size, the most extreme skaters of the new school become reasonable again, and styles of skateboarding take on a renewed sense of diversity.

With the help of Ed Templeton and Tum Yeto, Jamie Thomas, a Toy Machine skater, founds Zero. Handrails come back into style and Jamie Thomas is one of their principal promoters.

New shoe companies continue to spring up left and right. Tim Gavin and Kevin Dunlap found DVS, while Pierre André Sénizergues, the director of Etnies, starts up his second company, éS; a third, Emerica, would follow in 1996.

Specialized in sports programs, the cable channel ESPN launches Extreme Games, a sort of urban version of the Olympics where skateboarding takes place along side BMX and rollerblading. In the milieu of skateboarding, the news of the Extreme Games is met with both skepticism and enthusiasm. On one hand, hardcore underground skaters are afraid of being swallowed up by corporate entertainment, while on the other, the industry is open to this as it foresees that the new event could definitely aid its growth. The Extreme Games would undoubtedly contribute to skateboarding's fourth wave of popularity. In Rhode Island, Tony Hawk takes first place in ramp in the first season of Extreme Games. Chris Senn wins first place street here as well as in Münster, and is awarded the title of *Skater of the Year*. In ramp, first goes to the Brazilian Rodrigo Menezes, beating out Colin McKay and Mike Frazier.

While movie lovers discover through Kids, a Larry Clark film whose screenplay was written by Harmony Korine, a certain image of American youth associated with the world of skateboarding, Jason Lee retires from professional skateboarding to pursue a career as a professional actor. He appears this year in Mallrats, a film by Kevin Smith, with whom he will go on to appear in Chasing Amy (1997). Alongside Tom Cruise, Cameron Diaz and Penelope Cruz, he will act in Vanilla Sky (a remake of Alejandro Amenabar's Abre los ojos), directed by Cameron Crowe in 2001.

1996
Toy Machine brings out the video Welcome to Hell, which is highly representative of the tradition of East Coast of American skating,

and which also indicates an important turning point in the evolution of skateboarding. East Coast skaters had a knack for exploiting spots that West coast skaters wouldn't even notice in the first place. If tricks simplify, then the terrains upon which they are enacted diversify, just as certain skaters no longer hesitate to expand their repertoires in revisiting tricks too hastily buried by the new school, such as wall-rides and "wallies" (a wallride to air) and even "no-complies" (a trick which requires the placement of a foot on the ground). Donny Barley, Mike Maldonado, Brian Anderson, Ed Templeton and Jamie Thomas bring back into the foreground the simple pleasure of *riding*, doing series of tricks one after another and skating as fast as possible. Welcome to Hell is equally rich in gaps and handrails. It's also the first video since Propaganda (Powell Peralta, 1990) to include a female skater: Elissa Steamer.

Eastern Exposure 3: Underachievers, an independent production by the photographer and cameraman Dan Wolfe, is a perfect complement to Welcome to Hell. As the title indicates, this video is exclusively shot on the east coast, in New York, Washington and Philadelphia. Aside from Donny Barley (who also features in the Toy Machine video) the video brings together Jerry Fisher, Reese Forbes, Tim O'Connor, Jahmal Williams and Ricky Oyola, whose part is a particular stand out. From Dinosaur Jr. to Sebadoh to Pavement, Fugazi, Superchunk and Archers of Loaf, the indie rock soundtrack of Eastern Exposure 3 underlines its allegiance to the street tradition of the '80s.

Shot and directed by Spike Jonze, Mouse, Girl's new video, is the proof that the return to riding, so to speak, does not entail the decline of technique. Eric Koston, Mike Carroll, Rick Howard and the rest of the team learned how to become suppler and give a bit of breadth to their "flips." Switch-stance tricks are now done with a disconcerting finesse and mastery. Between certain parts, Spike Jonze inserts interludes which give the video its tone, the most successful being the one in which Rick Howard skates through a forest on a path made of plywood, covered by dead leaves, giving the impression that he is skating directly on the dirt (which is, needless to say, impossible). Drawing inspiration from Burnside, a group of Philadelphia skaters construct a concrete skatepark under a bridge (the FDR Bridge) without any authorization. The spot is known as Phillyside or the "FDR". Concrete skateparks are being built in the United States again.

American skaters boycott Münster. They protest the terrible state of its infrastructure and the zeal of the security staff. The Swiss skater Oli Burgin and the Spainard Ruben Raibal take first in ramp and street. At the Extreme Games in Rhode Island, Andy Macdonald is the winner of the ramp contest. In street, victory goes to the Brazilian Rodil de Araujo J.R. His compatriot Carlos de Andrade wins the Slam City Jam Contest in Vancouver, from this time forward, one of the most important international skate contests. After Mike Carroll, Eric Koston is the second skater from Girl to receive the title of *Skater of the Year* from Thrasher.

The Dogtown archivist, Glen E. Friedman publishes a sequel to his first book Fuck you Heroes. In Fuck you Too, the skate photos cover a period from 1976 to 1985. Fuck you Too contributed to the establishment of this chronology of skateboarding.

1997

After many years of effort, Jim Fitzpatrick and the IASC (International Association of Skateboard Companies) succeed in legally classifying skateboarding as a hazardous activity. The practitioners of such an activity recognize and assume responsibility for the potential risks they run. The AB 1296 law now protects the owners and managers of skateparks against any possible legal action in the event of an accident. This legislative reform will help considerably to encourage the construction of a new wave of concrete skateparks in the United States.

From 1995 on, Steve Rocco and Marc McKee market the visual identity of World Industries and Blind toward the ever-increasing influx of young skaters. Rodney Mullen leaves Plan B when Steven Rocco offers to help him start up his own company, A Team, whose first riders include Daewon Song, Marc Johnson, Chet Thomas, Gershon Mosley and Dave Mayhew. Giant launches Destructo, a new brand of trucks, which immediately comes to rival Thunder, Independent and Venture.

About thirty skaters now have a shoe named for them. Shoes are no longer bought only by skaters and the royalties earned by signature shoes are much more significant than a pro-model deck. Adidas, determined not to miss out on such a market, brings out two signature models, the Mark Gonzales and the Lance Mountain.

Well known on the French scene, the Lyon-based skater Jérémie Daclin founds Cliché, one of the first French skateboard companies. French and European companies would go on to multiply over the next few years, offering local skaters the possibility to support companies (and therefore the skaters) on a local and national level. Lacking the import taxes of American hardware, French boards are cheaper than boards from the United States. Cliché's reputation, whose team includes skaters as talented as Javier Mendizabal, J.-J. Rousseau and (later) Lucas Puig, would spread as far as the United States. The quality of Cliché's videos, <u>Europa</u> (2000), <u>Bon appétit</u> (2004), <u>Freedom Fries</u> (2005) and <u>Hello Jojo</u> (2006) would also help their growing reputation.

In kind of belated homage to Pat Duffy, <u>Thrill Of It All</u>, Zero's first video (Jamie Thomas' company) focuses on hammers, which means any kind of trick provided that it is spectacular and dangerous; hammers essentially consist of handrails and gaps. These two kinds of obstacles, handrails and urban drops of every kind (from stairs to plots of dirt in parking lots), become a kind of genre skateboarding. Some skaters would even go so far as to film only handrails and gaps, transforming videos into simple collections of spectacular single tricks edited in rapid succession. In <u>Thrill Of It All</u>, Jamie Thomas attempts to ollie a gap that has since become known as the Leap of Faith. This consists of an ollie over several steps, a guardrail and then a gap that is about 5.5 meters (18 feet) high. His board basically explodes upon landing, but he himself gets off relatively unscathed. Given that tricks are more and more perilous, the falls are some times terrible and fractures are frequently documented.

Heath Kirchart, a young skater who rides for Birdhouse, pulls off a kickflip to backside lipside down a ten-stair handrail as well as a "lipside shove-it out" on a thirteen-stair handrail (he ollies over the handrail frontside slides down, and as he comes off it, he makes the board turn 180° under his feet). He also goes under the knife for a small operation on his knee.

Tony Hawk goes all the way around the *Loop*, a wooden ring constructed by Tim Payne, modeled on small car stunt tracks. This feat is evocative of certain precedents, such as when Duane Peters and Kent Senatore both pulled off the same trick in 1978 in a full-pipe, which ended in a capsule. On a specially built ramp, Danny Way applies himself to breaking and setting a number of world records, starting by an aerial of 5 meters (16 feet) high. He also drops into the ramp from a helicopter. The exclusivity of this day is vouchsafed to Transworld magazine. But they were of course not aware of a hidden, spy photographer, Dan Sturt, who offers his shots to Thrasher. Thus does Transworld lose exclusivity to the images.

The renewal of interest in skateboarding can be gauged by the appearance and return of several specialized magazines: the legendary Skateboarder in the United States, Tricks, Freestyler (a magazine about skateboarding and snowboarding) and Sugar in France.

For their third season, and to the extent that skaters take on the status of superheroes, the Extreme Games becomes the X-Games. Tony Hawk wins vert, Andy Macdonald takes first in street. In Münster, first goes to Macdonald in vert while Willy Santos wins street.

Patty Segovia organizes the first female contest since the '70s, entitled the All Girl Skate Jam. Cara-Beth Burnside and Elissa Steamer respectively win ramp and street.

For the first time ever, Thrasher's *Skater of the Year* is not given to an American, but to a Brazilian, Bob Burnquist. Burnquist is part of a new generation of very technical ramp skaters who, in the tradition of Danny Way and Colin McKay, master switch-stance and tricks of street origin. Although ramp is no longer even shown in videos, the X-Games help put the form back on the radar.

In a New York gallery, Thread Waxing Space, Aaron Rose (himself the founder of the once fashionable Alleged Gallery) organizes The Shred Sled Symposium. Offering more than a mere history of skateboarding, the 196 pristine and unused skate decks that compose this exhibition also function as a retrospective of graphics produced by artists from the world of skateboarding. The exhibition also features wall drawings by Thomas Campbell, Phil Frost, Mark Gonzales and Mike Mills.

Glen E. Friedman's photos are exhibited in London at the Institute of Contemporary Art (ICA). The exhibition, entitled

Fuck you All, features a selection from his two books of photography, Fuck you Heroes (1994) and Fuck you Too (1996).

1998
Nike attempts to enter the skateboarding market and launches an ad campaign whose slogan "What if all athletes were treated like skateboarders?" is illustrated with basketball nets that are obstructed by metal bars or a golfer is chased off the green by a police officer. Consolidated, an underground skate company, replies with the slogan: "Don't Do It." Nike would not break through this time.

While Tony Hawk and Chris Miller found Adio Footwear, the skater Matt Field starts up IPath, a shoe company close to the interests of vegans and Rastafarians.

In the heart of the Block Shopping Mall in Orange County, California, Vans opens the largest indoor skatepark in the world (14 000 m2, 150,000 sq feet); the park also features a slightly smaller replica of the famous Pipeline combi-pool.

The production costs of Birdhouse's new video, The End, hits the 100,000-dollar mark. Far from any low-fi aesthetic, almost all of The End is filmed on 35 mm. Tony Hawk and Per Welinder, two ex-Bones Brigaders, now owners of Birdhouse, thus re-establish the standard of Powell Peralta's first videos. Birdhouse gives each skater the freedom to entirely conceive his own part. In a nod to the historic Animal Chin video, Tony Hawk orders the construction of a giant ramp, equipped with a loop, from Tim Payne. Installed in Mexico, in the middle of an arena, the ramp is 15 m (49 feet) wide and 4.3 meters (14 feet) high (60 cm, 23 inches of which is vert). Hawk films his part, which shows the famous loop, in six days. With the help of Hollywood technicians, Steve Barra offers himself the luxury of being decapitated by an invisible creature while an alcoholic monkey abuses Andrew Reynolds. After having played the part of teenagers in a van that destroys everything in its wake, Jeremy Klein and Heath Kirchart skate in Armani suits. With the help of a jump ramp, they manage to skate hitherto unattainable obstacles, such the top of a gas station pump, a Blockbuster video sign and the roof of a bus stop. They literally end in flames and jump into the water from the heights of a bridge under construction. The video, which also features Rick McCrank, Bucky Lasek and Willy Santos, is a great success.

Nine years after his first victory, Tony Hawk takes yet again first place in ramp at Münster. Just in front of Arto Saari and Chris Senn, first place goes to Brian Anderson in street. In tight jeans and perfecto, Andrew Reynolds receives <u>Thrasher</u>'s *Skater of the Year*; he is not the only representative of the return of the punk aesthetic: Ali Boulala, Corey Duffel, Ethan Fowler, Tony Trujillo, Patrick Melcher and Ragdoll (among others) are rails proponents of this style.

The 150th issue of <u>Transworld</u> comes out in October. In addition to one of the first articles on Barcelona (it would not be long before the Spanish city replaced San Francisco as the skateboarding capital of the world), it features interviews with Jamie Thomas and Shiloh Greathouse. <u>Transworld</u> publishes a thirty-page chronology of skateboarding edited by Dave Swift. Very well illustrated, the chronology covers 14 years of the history of skateboarding, from 1983 (the year of the magazine's first issue) to 1997. This issue of <u>Transworld</u> contributed to the establishment of this chronology of skateboarding.

1999
Steve Rocco, Rodney Mullen and the various shareholders of World Industries sell the company for roughly 20 million dollars.

Rick Howard and Mike Carroll leave DC Shoes to found Lakai. The distribution company Four Star also launches a new shoe company, Circa, whose first model is a Chad Muska signature shoe.

The first version of the <u>Tony Hawk Pro Skater</u> video game comes out on Playstation. Beginning in September 1998, Tony Hawk aids in the development of the game for ten months. An elaborate combination of recording devices, sophisticated motion capture software, and an installation of 19 cameras helped Activision's technicians digitize Tony Hawk's movements, as well as some other skaters. Bob Burnquist, Steve Caballero, Kareem Campbell, Rune Glifberg, Tony Hawk, Eric Koston, Bucky Lasek, Rodney Mullen, Chad Muska, Andrew Reynolds, Geoff Rowley, Elissa

Steamer and Jamie Thomas are the thirteen skaters that players of Tony Hawk Pro Skater can play in the game. On par with the best sales of the Christmas season, the game notably helps render the vocabulary of skateboarding tricks more intelligible (or at least, more concrete) to the general public's consciousness.

During the X-Games best trick contest, Tony Hawk pulls off the first 900 (an air that consists of two and a half rotations) in the history of skateboarding. The media goes wild. It is a revolution for some, a useless trick for others who say that the beauty of a trick has nothing to do with the number of spins or flips. Whatever the case may be, it took Hawk 13 years to pull off a "900." Some of the greatest ramp-riders, such as Danny Way, Rob "Sluggo" Boyce, Giogio Zattoni and Tas Pappas have all unsuccessfully attempted the trick.

In Münster, while Bucky Lasek takes first in ramp, Brian Anderson wins for the second time in a row first place in street. He is awarded the title of *Skater of the Year* by Thrasher magazine.

"The Lords of Dogtown," a long article about the Z-Boys by Greg Beato, is published in the March issue of Spin Magazine. Told as he sees it, the history of Dogtown is thrilling and goes beyond the context of skateboarding. Extremely well researched, Greg Beato focuses on biographical details and certain psychological traits that make his article a text somewhere between a screenplay by Harmony Korine and a novel by Ken Nunn.

A group of Hollywood producers take an interest in "The Lords of Dogtown" and start contacting the main protagonists, offering to buy the rights to their respective life stories. Just as Stacy Peralta begins to worry about Hollywood possibly coopting the Dogtown story, the producer Agi Orsi contacts him and asks him to direct a documentary on the same subject. Afterward, Stacy Peralta would write a fictional, Hollywood script based on and supervised by the Z-Boys. Greg Beato's article has contributed to the establishment of this chronology of skateboarding.

The more they age, the more skaters become interested in their brief history. Michael Brooke publishes The Concrete Wave, The History of Skateboarding, an anthology of texts and accounts put together in the style of a magazine. The book chronologically retraces the history of skateboarding. The author divides that history into four successive waves: 1959-1965, 1973-1980, 1983-1991, and 1993-1999. The Concrete Wave contributed to the establishment of this chronology of skateboarding.

Dysfunctional, a book edited by Aaron Rose, comes out this year, and paints a multi-faceted portrait of skateboarding. Essentially composed of images, Aaron Rose's book nevertheless features a chronology established by the famous Craig Stecyk. Dysfunctional contributed to the establishment of this chronology of skateboarding.

From March 27th to May 21st, two sociologists and researchers from the CNRS (National Center for Scientific Research), Claire Calogirou and Marc Touche, organize at the art center, the Confort Moderne in Poitiers, France, Skate Story, a journey through the history of skateboarding. The exhibition is accompanied by a little book that recounts the results of their findings: Le Skate, un jeu, un sport, un moyen de déplacement. (Skateboarding, a game, a sport, a way to get around).

2000

The number of skaters in the United States is estimated to be 10 million, 3 million of whom are Californians. A hundred thousand boards and five hundred thousands wheels are manufactured each month. Largely based in California, the skateboarding industry generates 1.4 billion dollars in sales for retailers this year. DC earnings alone represent 84 million dollars (against 7 million in 1995). The X-Games have 27.8 million viewers.

Transworld magazine counts 180 concrete skateparks in the United States. One of the most important is inaugurated this year, the Chehalem SkatePark. Constructed in Newberg, Oregon with a budget of 300,000 dollars, the park covers about 9,000 m2 (100,000 sq feet). The companies that best incarnate this return to the source of skateboarding are Anti Hero, Black Label and Consolidated. After the progressive dissolution of A Team, Marc Johnson founds Enjoi. Rodney Mullen, who has just conceived the truck Tensor, becomes his business partner. Andrew Reynolds leaves Birdhouse in order to start up Baker. According to Pierre-André Sénizergues, the ex-pro freestyler and director of Sole Technologie (which houses the companies Etnies, éS and

Emerica), shoes represent 50% of sales in skateboard shops (the sale of skate materials strictly speaking rarely goes beyond 20%). Given the financial stakes, shoe companies place a great emphasis on the quality of their videos. That said, one of the best videos of the year is Menikmati, the video for éS directed by the French Fred Mortagne. Menikmati features Bob Burnquist, Ronnie Creager, Eric Koston, Rick McCrank, Tom Penny, Arto Saari and Rodrigo Texeira.

In Münster, Bob Burnquist and Eric Koston respectively take first in ramp and street. With a height of 113 cm (44 inches) the Englishman Danny Wainwright wins the Reese Forbes Ollie Contest organized during the Trade Show in Long Beach, California and establishes a new world record. Geoff Rowley, originally from Liverpool, who rides for Flip, is the first European to receive the title *Skater of the Year*.

Craig Stecyk and Glen E. Friedman co-author Dogtown – The Legend of the Z-Boys. The first part of the book, *The Original Stories and Selected Images*, brings together all of Stecyk's most significant texts and images originally published in Skateboarder between 1975 and 1979. The second, *Picture Archive Discoveries*, features a new selection of Glen E. Friedman's photos. The texts and images of this work contributed to the establishment of this chronology of skateboarding.

The book A Onda dura (which means both "hard wave" and "the wave that lasts") is published in Brazil. It traces the history of Brazilian skateboarding.

Matt Lynch and Steven Badgett, from the collective SIMPARCH exhibit their installation Free Basin at the Hyde Park Arts Center in Chicago. Free Basin consists of a wooden reproduction of a Californian pool placed on stilts. Viewers can walk under the bowl while skaters skate inside it.

In France, for the large, contemporary art exhibition La Beauté organized in Avignon, Vito Acconci and his agency (Acconci is an artist who has been working over the past several years on the model of an architectural agency) offer to build a skatepark. The project, however, never comes to fruition, the funding is insufficient and the artist never manages to find a form that pleases him. In an interview with Delia Bajo and Brainard Carey, he explains: "So much of the stuff we do looks like it could be a skateboard park, but when we were asked to do a specific skatepark, we couldn't do it! We either made a potentially interesting space, but not of much use to skateboarders, or we made a space that's very useful for skateboarders, but we had to ask ourselves, why are we doing this, why not just make it out of a kit of skateboarding parts? We never found that in-between space, how to reinvent a space and it skateboardable [sic]."

"Jamie Thomas" is the first song on the Blur guitarist Graham Coxon's first solo album. It's a four-line love song:
Jamie Thomas, Jamie Thomas, Jamie Thomas,
Jamie skates so nice and clean,
Wish he could be my toy machine,
He's a hero, I'm a zero, He's a hero.

2001

Under the name of Dreamland, Mark Hubbard and Mart Scott, the creators of Burnside in Portland, have become specialists in concrete skatepark construction. Brixlegg, in Austria, is the first European city to commission a park from them. The Cradle Skatepark is inaugurated in the summer. The cradle, a sort of vertical and empty concrete half-sphere, which the park is named after, is the first of its kind ; it allows one to carve (i.e. use the suppleness of trucks to turn while keeping all four wheels on the ground) very high on the over-vert to the point of pulling off a loop. Since Brixlegg, Dreamland has created other cradles, primarily in Oregon, in Port Orford (2002) and Brookings (2003).

After ten years of a more or less underground existence, Black Label brings out its first video: Label Kills. The mix of ages, diversity of styles and spots makes Label Kills an instant classic of the order of Welcome to Hell (Toy Machine, 1996). Team Black Label has young, highly-adaptable skaters (Adam Alfaro, Kristian Svitak, Ben Gilley…) and features a group of influential skateboarders from various periods of skateboarding: Duane Peters, Matt Hensley, Jeff Grosso, Mike Vallely, Omar Hassan, Neil Hendrix, Salman Agah, Jason Adams and Wade Speyer). While the parts of Jeff Grosso, Duane Peters, Matt Hensley and Salman Agah seem historical period pieces, Mike Vallely, Jason Adams, Wade Speyer and Omar Hassan more than hold their own against the new generation.

With the victories of the Dane Rune Glifberg (ramp) and the Frenchman Bastien Salabanzi (street), team Flip dominates Münster. It is the first time a Frenchman is a world champion in a category aside from freestyle. Another skater from Flip, the Finn Arto Saari, made notable from his appearance in éS's video, Menikmati the year before, receives the title of *Skater of the Year*.

Stacy Peralta is given the Director's Award for his documentary Dogtown and Z-Boys (co-written by Craig Stecyk) at the Sundance film festival. The film is composed of a collection of photographic and Super 8-film documentation and footage by Craig Stecyk, Glen E. Friedman and Don Behrns, combined with extracts from interviews conducted between 1999 and 2000 with the entire cast of the Z-Boys. Sean Penn's voice unifies these various materials and recounts the history of this band of teenagers. Tony Hawk's and Stacy Peralta's trajectories are notably similar in a number of ways. As Dogtown and Z-Boys comes out in movie theaters, Tony Hawk's autobiography is published: Hawk, Occupation: Skateboarder, written in collaboration with Sean Mortimer. Circulated by the X-Games as well as by his own video game, Tony Hawk's fame propels his book to # 18 on the New York Times bestseller list. Dogtown and Z-Boys and Hawk, Occupation: Skateboarder contributed to the establishment of this chronology of skateboarding.

Thrasher celebrates its twentieth anniversary by bringing out the masterful Insane Terrain, a two hundred page catalog which retraces the entire history of skateboarding in images. Insane Terrain's photos as well as its introductory essay "History of Skateboarding" contributed to the establishment of this chronology of skateboarding.

Ocean Howell (a pro skater who rode for Birdhouse in the early '90s) is the author of The Poetics of Security: Skateboarding, Urban Design, and the New Public Space, an essay on skateboarding and architecture centered on questions of public space. The text and the illustrations of this stimulating essay are accessible on the internet (http://bss.sfsu.edu/urbanaction/UA2001/ps2.html).

In the same tradition, <u>Skateboarding, Space and the City, Architecture and the Body</u> a book by ex-skater turned architectural historian Iain Borden, is published in Great Britain. Building on the theories of Henri Lefebvre (notably his book <u>The Production of Space</u>, 1974), the author describes and analyzes the practice of skateboarding in relation to architecture. In addition to academic texts, Iain Borden combed through an astronomical number of American and English magazines in order to do his research. He details the history of concrete skateparks in the United States particularly well. Ocean Howell's essay and Iain Borden's book contributed to the establishment of this chronology of skateboarding.

2002

Skateboard companies are more and more coveted by large companies. After the buyouts of Zoo York by Ecko and Cliché by Adidas-Salomon in 2001, Billabong International Limited, a company that is traded on the stock exchange, acquires Element.

All Nike needed was two letters to successfully enter the skateboarding market. When Etnies and Vans begin to divide their production into two categories, models for broad distribution, destined for the general public, and those sold in skate shops to skaters, Nike applies the same formula, limiting its distribution of Nike SB ("SB" for "skateboard") to specialized shops only. Nike also puts together a team of skaters of varying personalities and styles, which would soon include Paul Rodriguez, Chet Childress and Brent Atchley.

With the help of Alias Distribution, Ed Dominick and Kris Markovich launch 88 Footwear. The company's name is evocative of their favorite year in the history of skateboarding. Unfortunately, the number 88 is also known as the code number for certain micro, neo-Nazi groups (the letter H being the eighth letter of the alphabet). The company, which would throw in the towel three years later in 2005, nonetheless had the time to produce a great video: <u>Destroy Everything Now</u> (2005).

<u>Sorry</u>, Flip's first video, which was made by Fred Mortagne, is one of the most anticipated videos of the time. Mark Appleyard,

Ali Boulala, Rune Glifberg, Tom Penny, Geoff Rowley, Arto Saari and Bastien Salabanzi are at the height of their reputations. Nevertheless, and despite the cameo of Johnny Rotten as the presenter, the video lacks personality.

Some skate shops produce their own videos, and this year the surprise comes from the shop Coliseum in Boston: P.J. Ladd's Wonderful Horrible Life. The P.J. in question (who, however, is not the only skater in the video) is captivating and his part immediately sets him among the ranks of some of the most technical skaters in the world.

A new Pipeline largely inspired by the legendary skatepark is inaugurated in Upland. The full-pipe is 6.7 meters (22 feet) in diameter and opens up onto a bowl 3.65 meters (12 feet) deep.

Using whatever materials are available, Pontus Alv and his friends quietly and surreptitiously construct a small, concrete skatepark in Malmö, Sweden, named Savannah Side. More and more caravans set up camp around the unused land where Savannah Side is located. Skaters begin to share the spot with an ever-increasing number of homeless people, dealers and small time thieves.

In the spirit of the famous daredevil Evel Knievel, Danny Way has a *MegaRamp* built, with a drop-in ramp link to a giant launch ramp; this is itself connected to a quarter pipe (a half ramp), which is nearly 6 meters (19 feet) high. Danny Way sets two new world records: an 19.8-meter (65 foot) air in distance and another that is 5.58 meters (18.3 feet) high.

For the second consecutive year, Bastien Salabanzi takes first place in street in Münster. The Canadian Pierre-Luc Gagnon takes first in ramp just in front of the Dane Rune Glifberg and the American Andy Macdonald. The title of *Skater of the Year* goes to Tony Trujillo. This Anti-Hero skater represents a new generation of park skaters capable of recycling every style of the history of skateboarding, from kickflips to old school tricks such as the boneless and the lean to tail.

The first issue of Kingpin, a tri-lingual European magazine (English, French and Spanish) comes out in December.

Jocko Weyland is the author of The Answer is Never: A Skateboarder's History of the World which comes out this year from

Century Publishing. The academic side of Jocko Weyland, which translates into a textual precision equal to his pedagogical flair, is generally offset by the autobiographical side of the book; the book owes its charm and interest equally to the fact that the author, born in 1966, is an ordinary American skater who lived through the greatest eras of skateboarding. Welyand does not conceal his past; in the form of The Answer is Never there is something of Mike Davis' famous book City of Quartz. The Answer is Never contributed to the establishment of this chronology of skateboarding. Claude Queyrel puts the first version of Endless Lines on line (http://www.endlesslines.free.fr), a website that functions like an anthology of French skateboard magazines. The covers and the most significant articles (sometimes the magazines in their entirety) are scanned; for better legibility, the articles are also transcribed. From the first articles in magazines like Tintin and Pilote in 1966 to the 4th issue of Noway (November-December 1989), Endless Lines now covers twenty-three years of the history of French skateboarding. This website contributed to the establishment of this chronology of skateboarding.

The artist and skater Ed Templeton has a solo show at the Palais de Tokyo in Paris from the 3rd of October until November 17th. Entitled "The Essential Disturbance", the exhibition consists of photos, drawings and wall paintings. A catalog, The Golden Age of Neglect, is published to coincide with the show.

In the context of a project by the artist Hervé Paraponaris, the Fond régional d'art contemporain Provence Alpes Côte d'Azur (Frac PACA) in Marseille is transformed into a skatepark. The park was supposed to be accessible to skaters throughout the entire "exhibition," but, from the evening of the opening, the neighbors complain about the noise and vibrations produced by the skaters. Looking at the few uninteresting modules, constructed by one of the worst skatepark contractors in France, would remain the sole privilege of the audience of what was a very feeble exhibition. Paraponaris' project is accompanied by a small book entitled Roule ma ville (Roll my city), which brings together photos of skateboarding, some drawings and a text by two sociologists, Claire Calogirou and Marc Touche. Finally, Free Basin by SIMPARCH is exhibited in Germany during Documenta 11.

Based on a screenplay by Harmony Korine that was written around the same time as <u>Kids</u>, Larry Clark and Ed Lachman direct <u>Ken Park</u>. The film follows the lives of a group of teenagers, most of them skateboarders, in a small town in suburban America.

Avril Lavigne sings "Skaterboy," the story of a girl who rejects a skater because he's not good enough for her. Years later, she sees him on MTV; the young skater has gone on to become a rock star. The girl then regrets not giving him a chance.

2003

Taking advantage of the enormous success of Zero and the support of DC Shoes, Jamie Thomas starts up his own shoe company: Fallen.

Danny Way has a new version of the MegaRamp built at Point X Skate Camp, a summer camp for extreme sports (skateboarding, rollerblading, BMX, and motocross). The gap, the space that separates the launch ramp from its counterpart is between 15 and 21 meters (50 and 68 feet) wide. As for the quarter pipe, this time it goes up a height of 8 meters (26 feet). Danny Way is no longer content to merely jump the gap, he performs a series of rather technical tricks over it: combinations of rotations and flips that he sometimes does even in switch stance. New records are set on the 19th of June: an air that is 23 meters (75 feet) long as well as another that is 7 meters (23 feet) high, which is to say, 15 meters (50 feet) above ground. The MegaRamp sessions are documented in <u>The DC Video</u>, which comes out this year.

Concrete skateparks continue to be built. Among the most successful can be found at West Linn (Oregon), which opens its doors in the month of January (and which is also where Brent Atchley would film the beginning of his impressive part in <u>Elementality</u>, Element's video, released in 2005). Dreamland inaugurates its second skatepark in Lincoln City, Oregon. This one, which is entirely covered, features a cradle, and is about 2,500 m2 (27,000 sq feet) in size.

In the second video by Black Label (<u>Blackout</u>) which comes out this year, Omar Hassan films most of his part at the New Pipeline in Upland. Anti Hero, that has some of the best park skaters on its team (John Cardiel, Peter Hewitt, Tony Trujillo...), also brings out a video, Cash Money Vagrant, which is short and intense. Also noteworthy is Really Sorry, Flip's second video, whose team now includes P.J. Ladd.

2003 is a year rich in videos. The most memorable is without a doubt Yeah Right! by Girl (which also includes Team Chocolate skaters) made by Spike Jonze. It was worth the wait (it had been seven years since Mouse). In 72 minutes and 26 skaters, Yeah Right! goes on to rank itself with some of Stacy Peralta's best work. As in Mouse, some parts are divided by sketches. For example, Spike Jonze and his team took the time to patiently erase each and every trace of skateboards under the feet of a group of skaters, making them seem to levitate just above the ground. The choice of music, which is very diverse, is likewise of the first order and corresponds perfectly to the various styles of the skaters: Joy Division, Interpol, Nas, Happy Mondays, David Bowie, Michael Jackson, Public Enemy, Frank Black, Le Tigre, Funkadelic, Death In Vegas, Scarface, John Frusciante...

From the 27th to the 29th of June the Boost Mobile Pro Contest, sponsored by a mobile telephone company, takes place in Las Vegas. Tony Trujillo and Bucky Lasek, respectively victorious in street and ramp, both win the biggest cash prize to date in skateboarding contest history: $40,000. A little less lucky, Eric Koston and Pierre-Luc Gagnon get $20,000 each for their second places. It's Las Vegas coupled with the mobile phone market. Incidentally, Boost Mobile sponsors some skaters and places ads in magazines such as Thrasher. Pierre-Luc Gagnon (ramp) and Greg Lutzka (street) win Münster. Mike Appleyard is the third skater over the course of the last four years from team Flip to receive the title *Skater of the Year*.

In a style reminiscent of Larry Clark's films, Kimya Dawson sings on her magnificent album, My Cute Fiend Sweet Princess, "Hadlock Padlock," an intimate view of the streets of New York as she and her friend Jeffrey Lewis know how to tell it:
> Little David was learning to skate, practiced every single day
> kept falling and falling and falling but he finally learned
> [to ollie
> he wondered who he'd tell, thought he would tell Mel
> but Mel and all his other friends were in the county jail...

2004

While the VF Corporation, a giant of the textile industry, which includes several large public companies (such as Eastpak, The North Face, Wrangler and Lee Jeans) buys Vans for $396 million, DC Shoes absorbed by Quicksilver Inc. Sole Tech, DVS, Lakai and Fallen resist this wave of buyouts. Paul "P-Rod" Rodriguez is the first skater to have his own Nike model shoe. His contract of several million dollars earns him the nickname Paul Dollariguez.

A sculptural version of the pop artist Robert Indiana's famous work *Love* can be found at JFK Plaza in Philadelphia. It is for this reason that the plaza is commonly known among skaters as Love Park. Like the Embarcadero in its time, Love Park is a spot of international renown. Tolerated until now, the municipality decides to permanently forbid skateboarding at the spot, drastically enforcing their decision. Philadelphia skaters and DC shoes organize a protest during which DC's young CEO offers the city a million dollar check destined for the upkeep of Love Park. Fox News covers the event, and according to a poll, public opinion sways (but not by much) in support of the skaters. The municipality however holds its position and rejects the offer. DC makes it known that the check will still be available for the next mayor, provided that he or she, of course, decides to end the prohibition against skateboarding.

"This is not a videogame, this is every street skater's dream come true," is the slogan of an ad for Rob Dyrdek/DC shoes Skate Plaza Foundation, which is published in <u>Transworld</u>. This foundation, initiated by the skater Rob Dyrdek, is a skatepark construction company that imitates public skate spots, their forms as well as their materials (hence the name "Skate Plaza" meant to distinguish these spots from skateparks).

The Skate Plaza, which corresponds to the 3D modeling in the ad, is being constructed in Kettering (Ohio), Rob Dyrdek's hometown. Its inauguration would take place on the 11th of June in 2005.

In June, the authorities in Malmö destroy Savannah Side, Pontus Alv and his friends' illegal, DIY skate park. In two months and still without any authorization, Alv and friends build a new concrete spot, Steppe Side, a vast and quirky mini ramp, a side of which is closed in a half-bowl. Steppe Side features various extensions, bumps and hips.

The pharmaceutical company Tylenol, whose pain-relieving qualities are well known to American skaters, begins sponsoring. Its team of "alternative athletes" notably features Tony Trujillo. The day a park financed by Tylenol opens, there is one dislocated shoulder, a fractured elbow and two head injuries.

Vanessa Torres wins the first female contest in Münster. Bastien Salabanzi takes first in street for the third year in a row while Andy Macdonald takes first in ramp in front of Mike Crum and Neil Hendrix. During the Best Trick Contest, the Brazilian Sandro Dias follows in Tony Hawks' footsteps and pulls off the legendary 900. The MegaRamp appears in the X-Games. Under the name of Big Air, this contest quickly becomes one of the main attractions. Danny Way wins this year, but Pierre-Luc Gagnon, Andy Macdonald, Jake Brown, Jason Ellis and Bob Burnquist are determined to catch up with him.

With a 24-meter (78 feet) long air, Danny Way sets a new world record. Thrasher magazine awards him the title of *Skater of the Year* for the second time.

Following a disagreement with the AOL TIME WARNER group, who own Transworld magazine, three of its most important collaborators, J. Grant Britain, Atiba Jefferson and Dave Swift, leave to found The Skateboard Mag. The first issue of this very serious magazine comes out in March while Big Brother stops being published this year.

After Tony Hawk, Rodney Mullen is the second skater to publish his autobiography. Like Occupation: Skateboarder, The Mutt: How to Skateboard and Not Kill Yourself, is written in collaboration with Sean Mortimer. Mullen's autobiography contributed to the establishment of this chronology of skateboarding. Independent brings out Built to Grind, 25 Years of Hardcore Skateboarding from the Archives of Independent Truck Company. The story of Independent Trucks offers a panoramic view of the history of skateboarding and its most rock'n'roll side, which is documented here. Built to Grind contributed to the establishment of this chronology of skateboarding.

Disposable, a History of Skateboard Art, which is edited by Sean Cliver, is published. This 244-page book, printed entirely in color, contains reproductions of more than 1,000 boards from the '70s through to the present. The information compiled by Sean Cliver, himself a graphic artist for Powell Peralta, World Industries and Birdhouse, is of a remarkable precision. Disposable contributed to the establishment of this chronology of skateboarding.

Justin Hocking, Jeff Knutson and Jared Jacang Maher are responsible for a small book entitled Life & Limb. With a preface by the author of The Answer is Never (2002), Jocko Weyland, this anthology of skateboard literature, brings together selections from a group of twenty skaters including Mark Gonzales, Ed Templeton, Scott Bourne, Dave Carnie and Niall Neeson.

At the request of the city of San Juan in Puerto Rico, Vito Acconci and his agency conceive a new skatepark project: A Skate Park that Glides the Land & Drops Into the Sea whose inauguration would be projected for 2005 (but, to my knowledge, the project has yet to start).

An exhibition conceived by Aaron Rose and Christian Strike opens at the Contemporary Art Center in Cincinnati: Beautiful Losers : Contemporary Art and Street Culture. Claiming the influence of the Beat Generation and Pop Art, Beautiful Losers features some big names from art history (Andy Warhol, Jean-Michel Basquiat, Keith Haring, Robert Crum) and a new generation of artists (all medias represented) close to urban culture (which they document or draw inspiration from): Thomas Campbell, Henry Chalfant, Larry Clark, Cynthia Connolly, Garry Scott Davis, Brian Donnelly, Cheryl Dunn, Futura, Shepard Fairey, Glen E. Friedman, Phil Frost, Mark Gonzales, Tommy Guerrero, Evan Hecox, Jo Jackson, James Jarvis, Andy Jenkins, Chris Johanson, Spike Jonze, Margaret Kilgallen, Harmony Korine, Geoff McFetridge, Barry McGee, Ryan McGinley, Ryan McGinness, Ari Marcopoulos, Mike Mills, Raymond Pettibon, Steve Powers, Pushead, Terry Richardson, Clare E. Rojas, Tony Silver, Craig Stecyk, Ed Templeton, James Todd, Romon Yang and Tobin Yelland.

The exhibition travels to the Yerba Buena Center for Arts in San Francisco (at the same time as SIMPARCH'S Free Basin). Before traveling to France (Lille, 2006), Beautiful Losers would be presented at Newport Beach (Orange Country Museum of

Art) in 2005. A 256 page catalog of the same name accompanied the exhibition.

2005

In its May issue, Thrasher publishes a long interview with Danny Way that concentrates his injuries. Since 2000, Danny Way has undergone seven operations on his left knee (three of which were reconstructive) and two others on a shoulder. He uses the best surgeons in the United States and Canada and owns his own gym, which is specially equipped for his rehabilitative needs.

Are You Alright? is a video produced by Transworld that documents a small group of skaters as they travel across the United States in a luxury camper. As they grow more and more tired, the skaters take greater risks and injure themselves more and more. The worst fall is taken by a skater nicknamed Danger, who, on coming out of the hospital, can no longer remember the beginning of the trip. Danny Way organizes a visit to the pharmaceutical aisle of a department store and gives a lecture to the rest of the team on the bandages of every kind, aloe vera creams and super strong pain relievers. The group goes to the checkout with a small mountain of articles. Danny Way's dressing doesn't quite work, so he decides to stop by a clinic for a (filmed) puncture. He foregoes a period of convalescence; he says to himself, no time to waste, they have a video to make, that's what Transworld is paying them for.

The installation of a MegaRamp in China begins in June. The launch ramp, which is now 36 meters (118 feet) high, allows Danny Way to gather enough speed to make it over the Great Wall on the 9th of July. But the evening before, during an attempt, Danny Way injures his ankle and the event, impressive as it is, is not a complete success. He does five backside 360s over the Wall, but can't manage to pull off an air, which should follow on the quarter-pipe (this time a height of 9.75 meters (32 feet). It seems probable that Danny Way, DC shoes and Quicksilver (the event's sponsors) would not have excluded the possibility of the Great Pyramids in Egypt had the Egyptian market represented as much potential as the Chinese market.

Catherine Hardwicke's The Lords of Dogtown comes out in movie theaters, but doesn't stay for long. Despite the active participation of the primary protagonists of Dogtown, such as Stacy

Peralta (who wrote the screenplay), Tony Alva, Jay Adams, Jim Muir and Skip Engblom, the film never gets beyond the format of a basic American film, rendering its interesting subject banal by cutting important scenes and concentrating instead on irrelevant detailsw. The film is a far cry from Greg Beato's article in Spin Magazine.

In October, Kingpin magazine brings out its 24th issue. On page 54 of the French edition, one can read the beginning of a very interesting article on the evolution of skateboarding and one of the most intelligent aspects of this pastime. The article is unsigned:
"At present, it would seem that the limits of what can be done on skateboard have been reached. Or maybe not entirely, but the fact of adding one or two stairs to railings every year doesn't make much sense, in the long run [...]. A traditional terrain of innovation, that of high tech, is perhaps more likely to continue to evolve, but after some video parts redefine the current limits – such as P.J. Ladd in Coliseum (P. J. Ladd's Wonderful Horrible Life, 2002), Marc Johnson in Yeah Right! (Girl, 2003), Daewon Song and Rodney Mullen in Round 3 (Almost, 2005) or Ronnie Creager in What If? (Blind 2005) to mention but a few –, how many more people will be able to take up the challenge? [...] This time, however, it's the kind of spots that make for revolutionary changes... A little like its origins, when the skateboard came out of the sea and landed on the asphalt, and the ground in general represented a completely unexploited territory, these recent years have seen a rebirth of interest in new terrains."

Experimentation and exploration are some of the most important parts of skateboarding. Another is the imagination, the "what can I do with this?" For the past several years, skaters take more and more trips and expand the frontiers of skateboarding. Magazines and videos document destinations like Mongolia, Greece, Morocco and Israel. Some travel in time, looking for historic but forgotten spots: abandoned skateparks, sometimes half-covered with dirt, pipelines hidden in the desert or in obscure suburbs. Others have become specialists of cracks in the cement, or some unexplored end of a sidewalk and make a spot out of almost nothing. It is sometimes the same people who, after the model of Burnside, construct under a bridge or on a piece of dead land, the first concrete beginnings of a future skatepark.

Still, in the month of October, the 71st issue of Freestyler magazine comes out and is accompanied by a video, which perfectly illustrates Kingpin magazine's ideas. Created by the Swedish skater Pontus Alv, The Strongest of the Strange, whose title comes from a Bukowski poem, functions both as a documentary and an artist's video. The Strongest of the Strange is not just a simple, heterogeneous collage of skaters, tricks and music, like Yeah Right! (Girl, 2003), but proposes what we all have the right to expect from every video: a singular vision of skateboarding.

The 300th issue of Thrasher comes out in November. The magazine does not go back over the history of skateboarding in this issue, but leaves to the most enthusiastic readers the task of putting together, according to their capability, the most detailed of chronologies.

A CHRONICLE OF SKATEBOARDING 2005–2009

2005
Paul Schmitt's factories produce 4,000 decks a day, which is to say, three decks a minute. This year they celebrate the production of their 10 millionth deck. Very concerned with environmental questions and an ecological conception of skateboarding, Schmitt presses his first bamboo decks.

With the financial support of Syndrome Distribution, Danny Way and Colin McKay re-start Plan B. P.J. Ladd and Paul Rodriguez, two current stars of street skating, leave their respective sponsors (Flip and Girl, the trendiest companies at the time) to join Plan B. Ryan Gallant is also part of the initial team, he would soon be joined Pat Duffy, Jeremy Rogers as well as the MTV reality star Ryan Scheckler. Darrell Stanton and Brian Wenning would soon spend a bit of time riding for Plan B.

Edmund Bacon, the architect of Love Park in Philadelphia, dies at the age of 95. Director of the City Planning Commission from 1949 to 1970 and author of Design of Cities (1967), Bacon sided in 2002 with the skaters when the city prohibited skateboarding in Love Park. In addition to giving speech in favor of the skaters,

Edmund Bacon, as a sign of protest, rode a skateboard across the plaza. In 2003, he said: "I don't think skateboarders have yet learned how to make themselves part of ongoing society. And they have allowed themselves through the media and through the actions of old and perverted people to be categorized as dirty, irresponsible, knocking down old ladies, and as a public nuisance, and it is the absolute reverse. It's really one of the most wonderful examples of their having created the whole thing themselves."

2005 is the year of skate plazas. These are streetparks, which is to say, skateparks that seek to reproduce characteristics of urban spaces rather than the transition of Californian pools; the concept is less innovative than it might seem. The originality of the skate plaza cannot be located in the classical opposition of street and transition, it can be found rather in the fact of being inserted in the urban fabric of a given location itself. The very idea of the "Park" tends to disappear. This new skateboarding space is not marginalized or preserved. The Ursulines skatepark in Brussels, which possesses a bowl, is a perfect example of a skate plaza. The collective Brusk, who initiated the project, conceived the space for skateboarding, but not exclusively. The end result is a skatepark that progressively dissolves into the public space (or inversely, a public space that is progressively transformed into a skatepark). The Ursulines square testifies to one of skateboarding's lessons: the refusal to let spaces be mono-functional, and the refusal to let spaces dictate how they should be used.

This year skate plazas are inaugurated in Vancouver (Canada), Milton Keynes and Middlesbrough (United Kingdom), and in Kettering, Ohio. Middlesbrough features replicas of famous street spots such as the MACBA gap in Barcelona, the semi-circular stairs in Love Park, and even the ledges on Pier 7 in San Francisco.

Jamie Thomas made no mistake when, in 2002, he named Zero's new video <u>New Blood</u>, letting Chris Cole have the final part. Chris Cole belongs to the school of very technical skaters who learned how to adapt tricks generally done on benches and ledges to handrails. <u>Thrasher</u> awards him the title *Skater of the Year*. He is also voted the 2005 readers' favorite by <u>Thrasher</u>'s primary competitor, <u>Transworld</u> magazine. Despite any differences the two magazines may have, they both agree on Chris Cole.

While Zero's image is attenuated by its commercial success (maybe also by Jamie Thomas' open Christianity, which is not at all suitable for the kind of rebels skateboarders tend to be), Baker skateboards now incarnates the new "hardcore" team: railings, gaps, slim jeans, beer, and rock and roll (the list is hardly exhaustive and should not exclude, above all, hip-hop). The videos that come out this year include Skate More (DVS) and What if? (Blind), in which the extremely technical parts of Daewon Song and Ronnie Creager are of particular note. Transworld magazine awards its annual best video award to Baker 3. The contrast between Baker's videos and those of Yeah Right! or even those made by Transworld magazine is analogous to the contrast of H-Street's low-fi quality and the high production values of Powell Peralta and Santa Cruz's videos in the '80s and '90s: in other words, the difference that exists between a four-track garage recording system and a professional sound studio. What makes the difference with Baker 3 is not the quality of its production, but rather its team, which is led by the much admired Andrew Reynolds: Erik Elligton and Jim Greco (recent fugitives of Zero), the facetious Australian Dustin Dollin and younger recruits such as Kevin "Spanky" Long, Bryan Herman or Antwuan Dixon.

Every Tuesday at 8 pm on NBC, Jason Lee plays the main character of the successful sitcom My Name is Earl, created by Gregory Thomas Garcia and produced by 20th Century Fox Television.

2006

According to the National Sporting Goods Association, skateboarding represents an annual market in the United States of 76.1 million dollars (down 2% from 2005).

In an editorial in The Skateboard Mag, Dave Swift estimates the number of professional skates to be more than two hundred; but he does not take into account all the pros who ride for European companies: Blueprint, Death, Landscape, and Heroin in England, Antiz and Trauma in France, Alai and Jart in Spain, Mob in Germany, 5th District in Switzerland and Yama in Austria, not to mention others.

After fifteen years of existence, Lance Mountain is finally obliged to close down The Firm. Bob Burnquist, Rodrigo Texeira and even Lance Mountain are all recruited by Flip, whose team is being totally restructured. Alex Chalmers and Bastien Salabanzi have already left it and Arto Saari would soon quit to ride for Alien Workshop.

Often with the help of a distributor, skaters continue to launch their own companies: Rasa Libre (Matt Field), 1031 (Kristian Svitak), Crimson (Kris Markovich), Traffic (Ricky Oyola), and Hopps (Jahmal Williams). The impact of the companies varies as much as their life spans.

Since getting out of prison in 2004, the charismatic Christian Hosoï has taken a bit of time to put Hosoï skateboards back on its feet. He starts by re-issuing his singularly shaped pro-model, the Hammer Head; with its nose in the form of a hammerhead shark and its tail shaped like a fish's tail, it is one of the most emblematic boards of the '80s. Hosoï hooks back up with Sergie Ventura (who rode for Hosoï at the beginning of the '90s) and also signs up Lincoln Ueda and the Italian Daniel Cardone.

The reemergence of concrete skateparks, the renewed interest in skateboard memorabilia nourished by E-bay, documentaries on skateboard legends, and historical books of all kinds, fuel the nostalgia of thirty- and forty-year-olds for their former skate years. Many get boards and start skating the bowls that are built close to their homes; some of them, although rarer, go so far as to pay up to $6,000 for pristine vintage boards.

Following Black Label, other companies such as Santa Cruz, start "Veteran Divisions" of teams featuring skaters 40 years of age or older. Santa Cruz, Powell, as well as Madrid and Gordon & Smith take advantage of the situation to re-issue their most famous models. Tired of manufacturing nearly identical decks, this return to the '80s gives many different companies the opportunity to vary the shapes of their boards according to their use (e.g., cruising, vert, etc).

In Barcelona, in what has become in just a few years the world capital of skateboarding, skaters protest against a new law that treats skateboarding on public sidewalks with the same severity as prostitution, begging and public drunkenness. Although the law was voted in, it seems that skaters are not the priority of the forces of order. In Los Angeles, however, the "week spots," which is to say, spots skateable during the week, have become almost non-existent. Professional skaters begin to travel more, Eastern Europe, Australia and China being some of the more popular destinations.

The largest skatepark in the world is inaugurated in New Jiangwan City, on the periphery of Shanghai. Designed by an Australian firm (Convic) and financed by an international textile group (SMP), the construction of SMP skatepark costs more than 26 million dollars. Without counting the 52 m (170 ft) wide ramp, whose height varies from 3.9 m (12.8 ft) to 5.1 m (16.7 ft) with extensions going to up 7 m (23 ft) and a 2000 sq m (21,000 sq ft) street space, destined for events such as the X-Games (accompanied by bleachers capable of hosting an audience of up to 5,000 people), the concrete part of the park is spread over 4,500 sq m (48,000 sq ft), and features no less than seven bowls of varying types and shapes. There are two full-pipes of different diameters perpendicularly linked to one another, the largest of which is closed by a Cradle. With a surface of 1400 sq m (15000 sq ft), and heights between 3 (10 ft) and 5 m (16 ft), the Mondo Bowl is gigantic.

Far from the "extreme" approach of the Shanghai park, the second skate plaza supervised by Rob Dyrdek is inaugurated in Shreveport, Louisiana.

Winnipeg, Canada, also celebrates the inauguration of its skatepark, The Forks. This park features a complex of bowls (8,000 sq ft) and a 44,000 sq ft skate plaza. In Winnipeg and elsewhere, a new generation of "paysagé" (landscaped) skateparks (to borrow an expression very much in vogue in the municipalities and architecture studios) is no longer limited to vast expanses of concrete, but also includes trees and expanses of grass. The Forks is well endowed with banks; somewhere between ledges and quarter-pipes, they are currently one of the most popular kinds of spots to film in videos. But beyond the more traditional forms of a skate plaza, the Winnipeg park also possesses what one would be tempted to consider as the first replica of a public work of art: a kind of undulating ribbon of concrete, which seems to detach itself from the ground and ride up into a vertical wall. It is certainly not a replica of a particular work (although one never knows), but rather a generic version of public sculpture.

In the United States, skaters complain about being forced to wear pads and protection in most parks. Californians have great expectations for their current senator, Bill Morrow, who would like to have skateboarding legally classified as a "full hazardous recreational activity," which would in turn completely exonerate municipalities of any responsibility with regard to accidents in their skateparks.

In 2001, Don Nguyen was the first skater to ollie over the twenty stairs at El Toro High School in Orange County (California), a spot well known among handrail buffs. On YouTube and all the skateboard sites, images are looped of a perfect kickflip executed over the same set of stairs by a young, almost unknown amateur Dave Bachinsky.

Chris Cole takes first place in the X-Games, beating out Ryan Sheckler and Andrew Reynolds. The Brazilian Sandro Dias wins first in ramp. On the MegaRamp Danny Way is victorious yet again. The two other steps on the podium go to Jake Brown and Bob Burnquist.

Due to lack of sufficient funds, the 25th edition of the Monster Mastership in Münster is cancelled.

First place for the 8th finale of the Quicksilver Bowlrider, which takes place in Malmö's new Stapelbäddsparken, goes to Daniel Cardone (Italy), ahead of the Spainard Alain Goikoetxea and the Swede Rune Gliberg. Not making it to the podium this time around, the Americans Omar Hassan, Benji Galloway and Chris Senn respectively rank 4th, 5th and 6th.

In the category of "Master Pro" in the second Protec Pool Party, organized at Block, a replica of the Upland Combi Pool, Chris Miller takes first place among a series of historically evocative names: Jeff Grosso, Steve Caballero, Lance Mountain, Tony Magnusson, Mith Smith, Steve Alba, Duane Peters, Pat Ngoho and Lester Kasai.

To the world of skateboarding's general surprise, Cliché is elected team of the year by Transworld magazine. After Flip (which rapidly moved to the United States), Cliché is the first European company to gain recognition in America.

Succeeding Chris Cole, Daewon Song is awarded the title of *Skater of the Year* by Thrasher magazine. For about the past 15 years, Daewon Song has been one of the most technical skaters around. In addition to his skill, Daewon Song skates fast, in many different spots and his tricks are often unexpected. He is also known for creating his own kinds of spots and obstacles, which are constituted by putting together picnic tables in schoolyards. Over the course of the past two years, Daewon Song has been in many vidoes: a part in Almost's video (Round 3, 2005), and another in a DVS video (Skate More, 2005). In Cheese and Crackers, produced by Almost in 2006, accompanied by Chris Haslam, they give mini-ramp skating a new lease on life by systematizing the "pop-out" (which is to say that they ollie out of liptricks rather than just drop back into transition). Never has the coping of a mini-ramp been so close to functioning like the lip of a ledge. To this resolutely street-style approach to mini-ramp skating is added an astronomical quantity of absurd tricks, which renders Cheese and Crackers a distant relative of Fischli & Weiss's celebrated Der Laufe der Ringe (1987), a succession of orchestrated accidents composed with various junk and materials that collapse like so many falling dominos.

Thrasher celebrates 25 years of existence with publication of a new book, Skate and Destroy, The First 25 years of "Thrasher Magazine." The book is organized in the form of a chronology of summarily annotated images, covering a period from 1981 to 2005. Among its innumerable photographic treasures can be found: a ten stair handrail by Natas Kaupas in 1987, the sequence of photos of Mark Gonzales ollieing what would thereafter become the Gonz gap, without forgetting John Cardiel's "backside 180 ollie" over the same gap in 1992 or Frank Gerwer's "kickflip" over the four long, Wallenberg stairs.

In France, Freestyler magazine is discontinued as of September. Its chief editor, Fred Demart, partners with David Tura, a former employee of Sugar, to found Soma magazine. Initially sold for 1 euro, the magazine would quickly become a free magazine, without, however, becoming a mere catalog of ads.

In the movie Wassup Rockers, the un-initiated discover that some skaters wear skinny jeans, listen to Punk and that this disgruntles local gang members as much as it disgruntles the older brothers of the young bourgeoisie in Beverly Hills.

Project 8 comes out at the end of the year. It is the eighth opus of Tony Hawk's video game series. Skaters who have been digitized this time include Rodney Mullen, Bam Margera, Bob Burnquist, Stevie Williams, Daewon Song, Mike Vallely, Paul Rodriguez, Ryan Sheckler, Nyjah Huston, Lyn-Z 113 Hawkins and of course Tony Hawk himself.

2007

After four long years of filming, Ty Evans manages to complete Lakai's video, Fully Flared, just in time for its premiere on the 16th of November at UCLA's Royce Hall. 89 minutes long (more than twice the length of any other video until this time), with 19 international skaters (Great Britain, Spain, France, Canada, and the US are represented), riding for one of the best teams at the time, and with an explosive introduction by Spike Jonze, all make it the major event of the year. Fully Flared is, in a way, the sequel to Yeah Right!, which is not so strange, given that Rick Howard and Mike Carroll are the founders of the two companies and feature in the two videos alongside Brandon Biebel, Marc Johnson and Eric Koston, who left éS in 2005 to start riding for Lakai. Fully Flared also marks the return of Guy Mariano, this being the first time he has had a solo part since his part in Mouse (Girl, 1996). The video likewise introduces two of the most talented skaters of their generation, Mike Mo Capaldi and Alex Olson, who would soon turn pro for Girl. In Fully Flared, Nick Jensen, Danny Brady, Lucas Puig and J.B. Gillet confirm reputation they originally earned in Blueprint and Cliché videos.

Since most video parts are generally as long as the song that accompanies them, the length of a video part is about the same as a music video. Although rare, double parts are parts that are long enough to feature two songs in a row. Most video parts are put to together like a "best of," and a medium length part of about four minutes is liable to represent several years of filming. Mike Carroll is now 32. A little more than 18 years after first gaining fame in early H-Street videos (those who saw Bootleg in 1991 can't forget his "360 ollie kickflip to smith grind" down a ledge or his "ollie one foot backside smith grind" on a handrail), he has a double part in Fully Flared, which confirms his status as a living legend. The same goes for Guy Mariano. As for the extraordinary Marc Johnson, he ends the video with a triple part 15 minutes long (a first in the history of skateboarding). The extremely precise statistical analysis carried out by a certain Dan Watson, which appears in the small booklet that accompanies the deluxe version of the Lakai video (Final Flare, 2008) informs us that with a total of 149 tricks, Marc Johnson's triple part represents about 20% of the total tricks in the video (849 in total).

At the beginning of the '90s, Mike Carroll, Guy Mariano, Eric Koston and Rick Howard largely contributed to the development of the most difficult tricks of the *new school*. The main characteristic of Fully Flared is its ability to continue to progress in the same technical way with tricks, in particular those performed on ledges, the tops of banks, or manual pads (a manual pad designates a flat, elevated surface upon which a skater rolls, balanced on two wheels. This trick is generically known as a "manual") and sometimes on handrails (which are rarely longer than ten stairs). Lakai skaters augment the possibilities of "flip in/flip out" tricks as much as they renew them, and contribute largely to bringing into fashion the double tricks in vogue at the beginning of the '90s. As indicated by its name, although a little limiting, "flip in/flip out trick" designates a trick, or rather a kind of amalgamation of tricks in which the skater executes a technical movement before and/or after any kind of "slide" or "grind" or even a "manual." This technical movement could be a combination of "flips," "varials" and even rotations of the body. In order to limit ourselves to just a few examples, let us note different variations of the "smith grind flip out" (Lucas Puig, Mike Carroll and Guy Mariano in particular), or Mariano's "blunt slides" and "noseblunt slide flip outs" ("noseblunt slide 270 nollie heel flip out") or Marc Johnson's "backside blunt slide big flip out").

In descriptive jargon, double tricks can be identified by the preposition "to" which indicates going from one trick to another. Here it is a question of changing the position of the skater's body during a "slide," "grind" or "manual" without letting the change interrupt or alter the progress of the trick. The most popular double tricks to do on ledges or curbs at the beginning of the '90s were "nose slides to crooked grinds" (the skater initially slides on the nose, and then he pops up into a grind on the front truck) and the "five O to switch crooked grind" (a "five O" is a "grind" on the back truck—from this position, the skater executes a pivoting movement so that the trick continues on the back truck, but backwards). In the same spirit, Marc Johnson pulls off on two linked picnic tables a trick that Willy Santos pulled off on a bench in the first Birdhouse video (Feasters, 1992): "frontside lipslide to frontside noseblunt slide." From a "frontside lipslide to switch crooked grind" to a "backside smith grind to backside nose slide," the variations are manifold and are sometimes repeated in the video parts of different skaters. One of the most memorable is without a doubt the "frontside tail slide to frontside nose slide" (a slide on the tail, with the edge of the ledge in front of one, then a 180 rotation so that the nose slides on the same ledge, but backwards, this time) by Mariano on a small, 8 m long (26 ft) wall.

Despite its strong team, Nike SB's video, Nothing but the Truth, doesn't measure up to Fully Flared. It's not that the parts are bad, on the contrary, but the intermediary parts as well as the uninteresting fictional envelope of the video both work against its success; fortunately, the DVD chaptering of the video allows one to pass from one skater to another without wasting time on so many bad sketches. Omar Salazar and Chet Childress's remarkable parts almost make one regret the fact that the Lakai video left so little space to simply riding and concrete skateparks and pools.

Other memorable productions from this year include Habitat's video, Inhabitant. The French company Antiz brings out ZMovie, which receives rave reviews in The Skateboard Mag, a rare honor for a small European video production.

Skateboarding continues to be historicized. Monographic documentaries become more common. After Mark "Gator" Rogowski (Stoked: The Rise and Fall of Gator, 2002, directed by Helen Stickler), Duane Peters (Who Cares? The Duane Peters Story, 2005, written by Keith Hamm), Christian Hosoï (Rising Son, The Legend of Skateboarder Christian Hosoï, 2006, directed by Cesario Montaño) and Jason Jessee (Pray for Me, The Jason Jessee Film, 2006, directed by Steve Nemick and David Rogerson), it's Steve Rocco's turn (The Man who Souled the World, directed by Mike Hill). The story of Rocco's ambivalent influence on the skateboarding industry's development from the beginning of the '90s onward makes this the most indispensible documentary of them all.

In the spirit of projects of the breadth of Burnside (Portland) and FDR (Philadelphia) or spots as quickly constructed by the likes of Pontus Alv and his Swedish friends, The Skateboard Mag establishes an initial, albeit non-exhaustive list of "DIY Spots." Among these guerilla constructions, among which concrete is the principal defining characteristic, are Marginal Way (Seattle), Washington Street (San Diego, California), Channel Street (San Pedro, California), Bordertown (Oakland, California), Rote Flora (Hamburg), and La Bassine (Marseille).

While with the inauguration of Pier Park in Portland (the first skatepark in a series of 19 projects in and around the city), Oregon confirms its status as the promised land of concrete, the Kona Skatepark in Jacksonville, Florida celebrates its 30th birthday. It is one of the largest survivors in the United States from the wave of construction in the '70s.

Chris Cole takes first place in street in the 13th season of the X-Games. In ramp and MegaRamp, victory goes to Bob Burnquist. Injured, Danny Way does not participate this year. In the absence of the historic contest in Münster, Germany, the most important contest of the year takes place in Prague. Bastien Salabanzi and Rune Glifberg respectively win street and ramp.

Thrasher's *Skater of the Year* goes to Marc Johnson; his triple, 15-minute-long part in Fully Flared made any other choice seem improbable. *Transworld's Awards* go to Fully Flared (video of the year) and Guy Mariano (street skater of the year).

Wanting to take advantage of the growing popularity of skateboarding, MTV launches two reality TV programs: Rob and Black, with Rob Dyrdek and his bodyguard Christopher "Big Black" Boykin (whose adventures had started during the filming of the DC video in 2003), as well as the controversial The Life of Ryan which depicts the personal and professional life of the young and talented Ryan Schekler.

The video Storm Sequence, which features a freestyler in slow motion against a background of a stormy sea, by the Australian artist Shaun Gladwell, is exhibited in the Venice Biennale. Later this year, while the Maloof Money Cup announces a $100,000 prize for the winner of the largest monetary prize in the history of skateboarding, Transworld magazine announces that an anonymous collector has bought Gladwell's video at a Sotheby's auction for the sum of $84,000.

Adapted from a novel by Blake Nelson, Gus Van Sant's latest film takes place in Portland in the environs of Burnside, here renamed Paranoid Park. The movie tells the story of a teenage skater responsible for an accident that cost a night watchman his life. This year, the film takes the special Cannes 60th anniversary prize. Despite the excellent cinematography, it is unfortunate that Gus Van Sant and his cameraman elected to use certain skateboarding gimmicks (fisheye lens and Super 8) rather than seek to innovate how skateboarding is portrayed. No error, however, was made in the choice of spots; to the Burnside parts is added a sequence in the giant pipe of Mount Baldy.

2008

This year, it's not the drought, but the global economic crisis that empties California's pools. Or this is in any event what an article in the New York Times explains on the 29th of December. Californian real estate agencies estimate the number of homes left empty by foreclosure to be at 10,000. "We have so many pools now we don't know what to do with them," says a skater in Fresno, a hitherto unknown situation for pool riders. Computer programs like Google Earth as well as sites like realquest.com or realtor.com help the most determined skaters to locate pools. Other specialized sites or blogs like skateandannoy.com also list certain spots. More often than not, ex-owners and real estate agencies didn't take the time to empty pools, obliging the skaters to do so, if they want to skate the pools. The writer of the Times article explains that, by doing this, the skaters counterbalance the illegality of their activities by an act beneficial to the local community, however unintentional it might be: in draining the pools, the skaters fight against the development of mosquito larva in the stagnant waters and the maladies, such as the West Nile virus, they are liable to breed.

Concrete skateparks continue to be built throughout Europe. Close to thirty years after the destruction of La Villette skatepark, Paris celebrates the inauguration of a covered skate park of 3,300 sq m

(35,000 sq ft). Despite the park's large size, the 4.7 million euro required to build it seems excessive to certain specialists. In France, this new park, built from prefabricated concrete modules reignites discussions about the advantages and disadvantages of shotcrete, as used in most American skateparks; this discussion actually goes beyond the question of skateparks, because the technique of sprayed concrete has never been developed in France as in the United States.

The first Krux Kickflips Challenges are organized in 2007. This rather monotonous contest consists of doing as many consecutive kickflips as possible. At the end the year, the record is held by the Dutchman Laurens Groeneveld, who did 566 in a row. The young American Zach Kral entered the Guinness Book of World Records on November 30th, 2008 for doing 1,546 kickflips. As stupid as the idea might be, not to mention the instigators and judges of such records, it's hard not to appreciate Zach Kral's thrilled smile in the photographs documenting the event.

The first edition of the Maloof Money Cup is organized in an amusement park in Costa Mesa, Orange County, California, from July 11th to the 13th. This contest boasts the largest cash prize in the history of skateboarding: a total of $500,000, $100,000 of which goes to first place in street, while $75,000 goes to first in ramp. This contest, which overshadows the X-Games, is the initiative of Joe Maloof, a multi-billionaire owner of a large chain of hotels and casinos in Las Vegas, several beer companies, and even a basketball team, the Sacramento Kings. A veritable streetpark, conceived by Rob Dyrdek with the help of some other professional skaters, including Andrew Reynolds, is built for the occasion. It is at once the most remarkable and most wasteful aspect of this contest: after three days of use, the park is destroyed. A giant ramp, designed by Jake Brown, is also constructed on the contest site. Paul Rodriguez takes first in street, followed by Nyjah Huston, Chris Cole, Ryan Sheckler and Darrell Stanton. First in ramp goes to Pierre-Luc Gagnon, who is followed by Shaun White and Bucky Lasek.

After his jump over the MegaRamp gap during the finale of the X-Games, Jake Brown loses control on his subsequent air on the quarter pipe and takes a terrible fall, plunging 12 meters (40 feet) down to the flat bottom. To the general surprise, after being surrounded on the ground by medics for ten minutes, Brown manages to get up and walk off the ramp. This year, Danny Way cedes first place in MegaRamp to Bob Burnquist. Ryan Sheckler takes first in street before Paul Rodriguez and Greg Lutzka.

Draconian laws against skateboarding are passed in Los Angeles. The few remaining spots are no longer accessible except during the weekend. Vis-à-vis this state of things, and also in order to improve upon the local, private skateparks owned by big skateboarding companies and reserved for their riders, Steve Berra and Eric Koston decide to buy a building and transform the ground floor into a private skatepark that they call The Berrics. The park is open to all their friends without distinction of the team they ride for. In order to keep a record of the sessions that take place at the Berrics, Berra and Koston conceive an internet site (berrics.com) that plays videos of individual or group skate sessions (the latter being organized according to team).

This is the beginning of Battle at the Berrics, which in just a few weeks, contribute to the international renown of this skatepark. Battle of the Berrics is a flat ground contest (no obstacles) based on the very popular model of "game of skate". The "game of skate" is a form of competition, a kind of match that skaters do rather spontaneously. In the offensive position, a skater performs a trick, which his opponent(s) must in their turn pull off. If the skater in the offensive position doesn't land the trick, he loses his offensive privilege, which goes to the next skater to initiate. If a skater does not manage to pull off the proposed trick, then he gets a letter. The match is finished when a skater spells the word "skate," which is to say, having missed five different tricks. Every trick must be pulled off on the first attempt, and, it goes with saying, without losing one's balance. In the defensive position, however, a skater who already has four letters is allowed two attempts on the final trick. The game has been institutionalized in the form of international contests over the course of the past few years by the company éS. In proposing this type of contest, Koston and Berra didn't invent anything new. What is remarkable, however, is the list of participating skaters. If the first edition of the Battle of the Berrics was so popular, it's because it brings together a selection of the best skaters of the time with a great variety of teams and generations. The firsts edition's 32 skaters (or rather 33 since Berra had himself replaced thanks to an injury in the second round) are: Clint Peterson, Paul Shier, Mikey Taylor, Benny Fairfax, Danny Montoya, Erik Ellington, Jimmy Cao, Bryan Herman, Daniel Castillo, Andrew Reynolds, PJ Ladd, Tyler Bledsoe, Eric Koston, Rob Dyrdek, Donovan Strain, Sean Malto, Joey Brezinski, Chad Tim Tim, Jeron Wilson, Mike Carroll, Atro Saari, Chico Brenes, Mike Mo Capaldi, Furby, Chris Roberts, Steve Berra, Johnny Layton, Billy Marks, Danny Supa, Brandon Biebel and Nick McClouth.

Responding to the availability of each skater, the contest takes place over the course of several months and each match is immediately broadcast on the Berrics' website. The finals take place on March 3rd 2009. The winner is Mike Mo Capaldi (Girl), while Benny Fairfax (Stereo) takes second and third place goes to Billy Marks (Toy Machine).

In France, on the occasion of DVS' ollie contest organized in Dôme, Nicolas Eustache does an ollie 103 cm (40.5 inches) high, while Vivien Feil gets up to 93 cm (37.8 inches) with a switch ollie.

Thrasher's *Skater of the Year* goes to Silas Baxter Neal, notably remarked for his part in the video Inhabitant (Habitat, 2007). Jake Phelps, the legendary editor in chief of Thrasher declares that, akin to Omar Salazar and Alex Olson, Silas Baxter Neal represents a new generation of "root street skaters" in the tradition of Tommy Guerrero. This can be understood as the opposite of the kind of very technical street skating in fashion over the past few years (Marc Johnson and Daewon Song). In this tradition, one could lament the fact that the title doesn't go to Dennis Busenitz, the extraordinary German skater who rides for Real.

In an interview that accompanies Fallen's first video, Ride The Sky, Jamie Thomas talks about a run-in with a night watchman. "I should have asked for the authorization and paid for the restoration of the ledge, but when it came down to it, I really enjoyed the little fight with the guard, even if he won this time." As prohibitions against skateboarding intensify, some companies go so far as to cut deals with the owners on which a given spot is located, whereby skaters are allowed to skate it if their sponsor repairs any damage committed to the spot. Fuel TV broadcasts, via the internet, Built to Shred, a program somewhere between Mac Gyver and The A-Team, in which the skater Jeff King builds all kinds of different spots in varying contexts.

In Bordeaux, the Octopus group proposes, with its "Sessions de chantier" (construction site sessions), a similarly temporary, build-your-on-spot approach that is not so far from Built to Shred.

After 12 years, Slap magazine turns into a web magazine, no longer publishing in a printed form.

Conceived by Jürgen Blümen and Daniel Schmid with texts by Dirk Vogel and Holger von Krosigk, Made for Skate, The Illustrated History of Skateboard Footwear is a work that is a lot less anecdotal than it might initially seem. The history of the shoe industry and its successive shoe models says a great deal about skateboarding's evolution. The iconography of the book is impressive while its references are precise—no surprise that this book should be co-published by with the serious Stuttgart Skateboard Museum. That said, the book's capacity to induce nostalgia in anyone over the age of 30 is incontestable. You see therein the shoes that you once wore as well as shoes you always dreamed of owning. In other words, incisive moments of nostalgia, which explains the growing number of re-issued shoes and decks.

Among the multitude of information, one learns from Pierre-André Sénizergues that, after studies conducted in the laboratory of the Sole Technology Institute, the impact on the ground after ollieing over twenty stairs is similar to that of a parachute jump, or that a fall from doing a handrail represents 17 to 18 times the weight of a skater.

Made for Skate contributed to the expansion of the second edition of this chronology of skateboarding.

2009
A new wave of pro skaters comes of age. To the large number of 30-year-old plus skaters are added a generation of skaters born between 1980 and 1990: Sean Malto, Mike Mo Capaldi, Alex Olson (Girl), Dylan Rieder, Grant Taylor, Omar Salazar (Alien Workshop), Billy Marks, Nick Trapasso (Toy Machine), Lucas

Puig, Andrew Brophy (Cliché), Benny Fairfax (Stereo), Chris Pfanner (Anti Hero), Nick Dompierre (Real), Tommy Sandoval (Zero), Chris Troy, Shuriken Shannon (Black Label), Torey Pudwill (Almost), Brandon Westgate (Zoo York), etc.

Bod Boyle, the president of Dwindle Distribution, announces the buyout of Cliché from Salomon, who was its proprietor since 2001. Owned by Dwindle, the French company joins a list of American companies, which includes Enjoi, Almost, Blind, Darkstar and Tensor. Al Boglio and Jeremy Daclin maintain their independence in terms of the artistic direction and team management; they will direct Cliché from Lyon, France. Their decks, along with all the decks distributed by Dwindle, will be produced in China according to a delocalization plan initiated in 2004 and supervised by Rodney Mullen.

With the creation the CTS allstar, a skateboard version of the famous Chuck Taylor, Converse enters the skateboard market. To celebrate the launch of the collection designed by Stephen Sprouse, Louis Vuitton brings out a limited edition skateboard deck also designed by Sprouse and sold in a case for $8,250.

During the filming of Video Days (Blind, 1991) in 1990, Mark Gonzales ollies the long four steps at Wallenberg High School in San Francisco for the first time. Twelve years later, Frank Gerwer clears the 7 meters (23 ft) of the Big Four with a kickflip; meanwhile, Jesse Paez (1992) and Diego Bucchieri (1998) had respectively pulled off a frontside 180 ollie and a backside 180 ollie. In 2003, Tony Manfre pulls off the first two switch tricks over the massive stairs, a switch ollie and a switch frontside 180. In 2004, Zero and Thrasher organize the first best trick contest at Wallenberg High School. On this occasion, Steve Nesser clears the stairs with a "pop shove it," Lindsey Robertson does a heelflip, Darrell Stanton a switch backside 180 and Andrew Reynolds a frontside 180 kickflip. A year later, Chris Cole does a 360 kickflip over the stairs, which can be seen in the video New Blood (Zero, 2005). On May 30th 2009, a new contest is organized on the Big Four. Marisa Dal Santo almost become the first woman to ollie this gap—she lands, but doesn't manage to keep rolling. This time Chris Cole pulls off a backside 360 ollie as well as a switch frontside 180 kickflip. Aside from a very risky "ollie disaster" on the last stair (which is to say an "ollie" in which the middle of the board intentionally hits the final stair), Mike "Lizard King" Plum, the king of tricks from any era, pulls off a backside one-footed ollie and ollie airwalk. The list grows with a varial heelflip by Jordan Hoffart, an ollie bigspin by Cody McEntire and finally a hardflip by Andrew Pott.

In June, the magazine <u>Soma</u> publishes a list of tricks pulled off over the most famous Parisian gap, the five Bercy blocks, which corresponds to about 15 stairs: 1999, backside 180 ollie by Jeremy Wray, kickflip by Andrew Reynolds. 2003: frontside 180 kickflip by Greg Lutzka. 2004: switch ollie by Zered Bassett. 2005: ollie one foot and switch frontside 180 ollie by Sierra Fellers. 2008: backside heelflip and backside 360 ollie by Andrew Reynolds, as well as a switch heelflip by Furby. 2009: 360 kickflip by a young French skater, Adrien Bullard.

From a list of 172 names, internet users are invited to select the next participants of Battle at the Berrics. The 32 selected skaters are: Chris Cole, Mike Vallely, Jamies Thomas, Dennis Busenitz, Lizard King, Heath Kirchart, Corey Duffel, Rick Howard, Chris Haslam, Nick Dompierre (who is eventually replaced by David Gonzales), Torey Pudwill, Jimmy Carlin, Josiah Gatlyn, Cairo Foster, Guy Mariano, Cesar Fernandez, Cory Kennedy, Josh Kalis, Lucas Puig, Greg Lutzka, Stefan Janoski, Peter Ramondetta, Mark Appleyard, Ben Gore, Paul Rodriguez, Kelly Hart, Gilbert Crocket, Kerry Getz, Nick Trapasso, Danny Garcia, Jerry Hsu and Kenny Anderson. The second edition of the Battle at the Berrics is inaugurated in June and begins with a match between Chris Cole and Mike Vallely, an exceptional battle rich in "handplants" (a trick popular in the '80s where skaters did balancing tricks with one or two hands on the ground and in contravention of the normal rules of the S.K.A.T.E. game).

This year, the Maloof Money Cup street park is designed by Geoff Rowley. Without being exact replicas, the obstacles that compose his park are made with similar forms and materials of well known urban spots: a square handrail located just next to Sunset Boulevard in Los Angeles; the big four from Rincon Middle School in San Diego; an inclined ledge from Barcelona; the manual pad from Pier 7 in San Francisco; the Brooklyn banks in New York, etc. Chris Cole takes first in street just in front of Tommy Sandoval and Nyjah Huston. In women's, first place goes to Leticia Bufoni, in front of Lacey Baker, Elissa Steamer, Amy Caron and Marisa Dal Santo. Alex Perelson, a newcomer in the little circle of ramp riders, steals first from two contest-winning veterans, Pierre-Luc Gagnon and Bob Burnquist.

In Lafayette Park in Los Angeles, Rob Dyrdek develops his first *Safe Spot, Skate Spot*, which is akin to a Skate Plaza, but just smaller, and located inside a public park. The logic of a skate spot plays upon blurring the boundaries between a recreational space and a standard public space: an open space with benches, low walls, and steps. Here, the question of alternate use actually goes contrary to what one would expect: to sit on a bench or use a handrail is to use a skate spot in a way that goes against its functional logic. If street skating is still the privileged domain of most skaters, this domain implies an experience or an awareness that transcends skateboarding itself. Skateboarding is an activity as much as it is an intuitive and corporeal awareness of the city, of its materials and forms as well as the social networks of which it is composed. Skate Spots offer skaters the opportunity to develop this same awareness of the city, in addition to that of traditional skateparks.

Shot by Greg Hunt between 2004 and 2009, Mind Field, Alien Workshop's fourth video since Memory Screen (1992), is without a doubt the best video of the year. More than Nothing But The Truth (Nike SB, 2007), Mind Field offers a better alternative for those who, in Fully Flared (Lakai, 2007) would prefer Alex Olson's part to that of Guy Mariano; a street style that is much more energetic, aggressive and fluid depending on the skater, but which adequately represents the team's young recruits: Dylan Rieder, Grant Taylor, Omar Salazar and Jake Johnson. With the participation of Jay Mascis and the various songs by Dinosaur Jr. used in the sound track, the general tone of Alien Workshop's video is evocative of Mike Vallely's celebrated part in Speed Freaks (Santa Cruz, 1989).

Coan Nichols and Rick Charnoski are the directors of a new documentary on the evolution of skateboarding in New York, From Deathbowl to Downtown, co-written by the author of the excellent The Answer Is Never, Jocko Weyland. This counterhistory of American skateboarding is narrated by Chloé Sevigny. At around the same time, <u>Sick Boys</u>, the film made by Mike McEntire in 1988 comes out on DVD.

In Europe, the director Philippe Petit has been following the travels of the Belgian skater David Martelleur for several years. With <u>Danger Dave</u>, it's possible to hope that Philippe Petit will put the apologetic monographs of his American colleagues to shame.

POSTFACE

The first edition of this chronology came out in 2006. When B42 editions offered to reissue the original French text, updated with a new section from 2005 to 2009, I didn't initially realize the implications of adding four years of history.

Despite the form, or rather the absence of form, presupposed by a chronology, and despite the neutrality of tone that I had imposed upon myself while writing, I wanted to give the story a beginning and an end, or to put in another way, an introduction and a conclusion. I borrowed the conclusion from an article in Kingpin magazine, whose points seemed to perfectly illustrate Pontus Alvs' video, The Strongest of the Strange. It was not my intention to say that nothing had changed in four years. And yet, still today, I can find no better way to conclude.

Since 2006, I have followed the evolution of skateboarding from afar, buying from time to time a magazine or a video that I knew to be indispensible, or almost. I devoted myself to other projects: a collection of photos of skaters riding public art (Riding Modern Art, from 2007 on-going), a film about the spaces of skateboarding culled from about forty documentaries and skate videos (Topographie anecdotée du skateboard, also titled Species of

Spaces in Skateboarding, 2008), research regarding Galieo's mechanics from the 17th to the 18th century, the experiments of which concerned gravity, the fall of bodies and the movement of small, metal balls along curves and inclined planes, all seemed to me to prefigure the involuntary experimentation of skateboarders.

While working on this update, my main anxiety was the excess of information. Between May and September 2009, thanks to the archives of the Parisian skateshop Nozbone, I consulted over a hundred magazines. With the help of the internet, and at the risk of losing myself in the details of daily chronicles, I complemented and cross referenced certain bits of information. Since any kind of exhaustive presentation was impossible, I sought to circumscribe events that seemed to me symptomatic.

Never had my enterprise seemed to me so lacunal, so full of gaps. Working on these last and final four years (to which I added a new version of 2005) gave me the feeling of editing hundred of hours of raw footage of a Cecil B. DeMille epic into a ten minute short. I now leave to the magazines, to the growing number of documentaries, blogs and the internet in general, the task of completing and filling out the gaps of this project.

THE FORBIDDEN CONJUNCTION

PROLOGUE

Skateboarding is a tenacious obsession for the those who began doing it early on in their teenage years. Forms created by skateboarding can be seen more and more in galleries, museums and some of the most significant manifestations of contemporary art. This fact, which some might see as a simple phenomenon of fashion, is nothing less than the outcome of a logical evolution: the young skaters who just twenty years ago infested public spaces and built mini-ramps in their backyards, are now of the age to exhibit in Documenta.

Skateboarding structures the world view of those who practice it. Despite itself, it engenders a reevaluation of spaces and materials otherwise taken for granted. Who, aside from an artist like Ed Rusha, would be interested in an empty parking lot?

I didn't immediately realize why I found certain works of art, such as Imi Knoebel's hermetic piles of boards, so striking at first glance. This paradoxical familiarity was largely the result of the value that skateboarding had trained me to accord to a nice piece of plywood, and which I inevitably brought to a pile of plywood leaning against a wall. In the street, the stockades erected for the construction of a façade or a shop window are always a source of happiness as they remind me of the smooth surface of a new skatepark. On the other hand, I have zero sympathy for old pieces of plywood which are soft, disfigured by humidity, and full of splinters.

The text that follows is in a sense an introduction to skateboarding. Certain artists may perceive skateboarding from the vantage of minimalism, while others from that of performance, and others still from the popular arts and crafts-- the important thing being that it resonates in one way or another with one. For my part, I have adopted the "Roger Caillois" point of view. But what is the relationship between Roger Caillois and skateboarding? To answer this question based on a single work, "Man, Play and Games" (1958, trans 1961), would certainly not suffice. It is, after all, not the most up-to-date text and there is something even a little outmoded about its tables, cases and categories. When I decided to use Roger Caillois as a point of departure for a so-called study of skateboarding, I pictured more the entire literary trajectory of the man rather than any single work. I am thinking of the Caillois of "The Writing of Stones" and "The Mask of the Medusa," of he who can transform the basic scientific principles underlying his research into literature. The Caillois who discovered and translated Borges.

My goal was simple: to write about skateboarding, and by doing so, appropriate for myself an activity which had occupied me in a quasi-obsessive way during my teenage years. I wanted to create a sense of order while attempting to communicate to others, especially those completely unfamiliar with this activity, the logic behind such an obsession.

Thus, while waiting for other texts featuring more elaborate forms of reflection, biographical details and factual descriptions, I here timidly propose this small offering: I would like to "weave" these few notes into a reading of Roger Callois' work. A small homage to a writer who promotes a way of doing, what he called a "diagonal science." This then is an essay to read as if it were a tale in waiting, or an introduction to an initiation.

INCURSION

> *There are innumerable and various types of games: board games, games of physical skill, of chance, open air, of patience, of construction, etc. Despite this almost infinite diversity and with a remarkable consistency, the word 'game' conjures up the same idea of leisure, risk and skill. Above all, it infallibly bears with it an atmosphere of abandon and entertainment. It is a source of relaxation and enjoyment. It evokes an activity devoid of constraint, and which is no less devoid of consequences on everyday reality. It is opposed to the seriousness of everyday life and is, as such, qualified as frivolous. Elsewhere, it is opposed itself to work as if it were a kind of lost or wasted time contrary to time well spent. Indeed, the game or play produces nothing: neither goods nor works. It is essentially sterile. At the beginning of each new game, and even if they played their whole lives, the players always return to zero, and in the same conditions as the first game.*[1]
>
> Roger Caillois

Roger Caillois classifies play or the game among four primary categories: competition (*agôn*), chance (*alea*), simulation (*mimicry*) and vertigo (*ilinix*). According to him, modes of playing can be situated between two antagonistic poles: the motive power (*paid*) and the all-powerful rule (*ludus*). After these primary categories, he couples them. Of the six possible conjunctions, two are fundamental, two are contingent, and the remaining two are antonymic or forbidden. That one of the two "forbidden conjunctions" best characterizes skateboarding (and more generally, any sport involving "sliding"[2], e.g., surfing, skiing, snowboarding, etc.)

---

[1] Roger Caillois, *Les jeux et les hommes: le masque et le vertige*. Gallimard, Paris. 1958, pg. 9. Citation translated from the untranslated introduction by Chris Sharp.

[2] "Sliding" refers to "sport de glisse" which is a specifically French expression invented at the end of the '80s, and could be literally translated as "sliding sports." The expression was originally conceived by a surfer, Yves Bessas, author of the book, *La Glisse*, published in 1982, whose subject matter dealt with a certain number of sports such as skiing, surfing, windsurfing, sailing, the flying wing, gliding, rafting, kayaking, canoeing, sledding, skateboarding, rollerskating, ice-skating, etc. "Sport de glisse" basically refers to "extreme sports," which is how it shall hereafter be known throughout the rest of this text (translator and author's note).

seems to indicate that games and the way they are played, just like art making practices incidentally, have expanded and become considerably more complex over the course of the last fifty years.

THE GAME AS ACTIVITY

The game is defined by Roger Caillois as an activity that is at once free, separate, uncertain, and unproductive: strictly governed by rules or make believe (the two last terms being almost exclusive of one another). Before anything, however, it is a form of recreation; whoever plays is free to play or not to play. A compulsory game is not enjoyed as a game, in the sense that to live, or survive, is not to play. The game is a separate activity, which is to say, "circumscribed within limits of space and time, defined and fixed in advance." (pg 9).[3] Whether the players measure their results against others or themselves, the outcome of the game is always uncertain, as to play is to surrender oneself to chance. The game is unproductive and in this way differs from any professional activity. The remunerated player (athlete, actor or other) no longer plays, he or she works; that nevertheless does not change the nature of the game. Governed by rules, the game is submitted to "conventions that suspend ordinary laws, and for the moment establish new legislation, which alone counts." (pg 10) In indulging in make believe, the game may accompany the awareness of a reality parallel to everyday reality, even of a total unreality.

Although there are numerous spaces created expressly for the activity of skateboarding (skateparks), it is above all an urban activity. More precisely, it is a practice "of the urban," in the sense that its terrain is really the city, or at least a montage of the diversity of the city's materials and forms. Contrary to this, hip-hop dancing (an example among many other forms of urban recreation) merely breaks down the walls between the space reserved for training and its representation. It limits itself to a tiny parcel of the overall urban space. Of public space, its adepts seek out the smoothest possible surfaces (marble, granite), with or without

[3] All page numbers in parentheses refer to Roger Caillois' *Man, Play and Games*. Translated by Meyer Brash. 1961. University of Illinois Press, Urbana, Chicago, 2001

foot traffic, covered and heated depending on the season. Yet while the skater may ignore numerous aspects of the city, he rarely limits himself to a single surface. He uses a variety of urban accoutrements (benches, garbage cans, fire hydrants, etc) as much as architecture (flat or inclined surfaces, stairs, curbs, etc). He inhabits and uses the city differently than a pedestrian or even a *flâneur* would. Skateboarding is always engaged in pushing the limits of the possible, at once dynamizing and destabilizing certain forms and objects conceived for rest and comfort (benches, stairs, handrails, etc). It is not a game that has expanded beyond its original terrain (as in the case of soccer in the street) nor is it an activity whose terrain was inserted in the city (a basketball court, for example, under an overground metro stop.

From the very beginning, skateboarding was a response to one of the main questions asked of urban space by its youngest inhabitants: how can one play in the city? Skateboarding originated from the encounter of a home-made sidewalk scooter and a surfboard. As it is practiced today, skateboarding emerged in working class neighborhoods of Los Angeles and around a small beach encircled by concrete in Santa Monica. This beach, located along the margins of Malibu, is in a sense the meeting point of two worlds, two immensities: the ocean and the city. Skateboarding, which was initially known as "sidewalk surfing," is the alternative to a day with no waves. These young surfers perceived the city as a new element, a natural playground of extraordinary complexity. Skateboarding is a game of discovery and adaption, its original terrain being that of the "off the beaten urban path." [4] In 1978, a sociologist spoke correctly of what he called "off the beaten path skateboarding," (*Le skate sauvage*) [5] because, akin to camping, spaces created expressly for such activities did not precede them, but rather succeeded them. What is more, the creation of skateparks, and more often than that, of minor skate terrains, [6] is

---

4 This is the expression used as the title of a work by Yves Pedrazzini, *Rollers et Skaters: sociologie du hors-piste urbain*, L'Harmattan, coll. "Changement," Paris, 2001. This idea of the "off the beaten urban track" (*hors-piste urbain*) was already present in the work of the sociologists Marc Touché and Claire Calogirou.
5 Jacques Carroux, "Le skate sauvage" *Esprit*, October, 1978.

6 I write it thus in order to register the difference between large and complex spaces constructed in either wood or concrete (skateparks), and those which are more common, and which are limited to a small patch of asphalt, where one might find a couple of ramps and modules. These more common spaces are often conceived as playgrounds for big kids who have yet to grow up.

not always perceived in the same way by all skaters. Certain among them relate to the emergence of these "artificial" terrains as the response to a real need, while others, on the contrary, perceive them as nothing more than a means to justify an increasingly severe prohibition of skateboarding in public spaces. Nevertheless, few would completely boycott such parks; the majority of skaters use them merely as a place to hone skills better served in the city itself.

Spaces reserved for games are classically separated from those of everyday life. It is only children who play in the spaces of everyday life. They transform them through the fiction of make believe or *détourne* them through the invention of arbitrary rules. Among adults, however, the gap between the world of games and that of everyday life is very real. The life of a responsible adult consists of a series of events that must be faced, or which one must struggle to avoid, whether one likes it or not. The game is the dominion of free choice *par excellence.* In order for a game to be a game, one must be free to choose at any given moment whether or not to play (any longer). The player chooses his own obstacle, an obstacle made to his or her measure, "Reality," wrote Caillois, "does not concern itself with such delicacies."[7]

To mix the pleasure of the game with the seriousness of life is indecent. "The game is a luxurious activity that presupposes leisure time. Those who are hungry do not play."[8] One wants to play, but only if everyone else plays, and if the place in which one plays is separated from those who do not play. Also, certain spaces reserved for playing seek to legitimize the game through luxury: I can play because I have paid my membership fees, I can allow myself to play here, because this space is not made for slackers." It's a question of the good conscience of those who play and demonstrate while playing that they have earned their right to relaxation through having paid their tribute of seriousness and of work (and their membership fees as well as for their brand new equipment) to society. Contrary to this, to play in the world of those who work is to expose oneself to judgements of the following

---

[7] Caillois. Ibid. pg. 25. Citation translated from the untranslated introduction by Chris Sharp.

[8] Ibid. pg. 24

type: "They play while we work." In such conditions, he or she who plays in the street is nothing more than either a rich kid or kind of slacker, the latter who let themselves be supported by the society they tacitly criticize through their laziness. Although caricatural, these two interpretations are not necessarily false, and one should not underestimate the spirit of rebellion that accompanies an activity developed at the same time as punk music. But among young adult skaters [9] (amateurs), public spaces and streets are terrains as legitimate as any other, while the practice of skateboarding itself remains a pasttime as separate from the skater's professional life as any another hobby. For the skater, then, skateboarding is at once spatially included in everyday life while also being temporally separate from it.

In a 1977 documentary on skateboarding at the Trocadéro, two children explain to the camera: "We skate when we want... and wherever... We always have our boards with us, and if we're bored at home, we go skating on the sidewalks outside. Meanwhile with any other sport, you have to go a club on a certain day, which, in the end, is a constraint." [10] A year later, Jacques Carroux wrote in the review *Esprit*: "It would seem that the success of skateboarding underlines while trying to remedy the difficulties of practicing sports in our cities, especially the big ones." [11] By appropriating as its space of activity the space of everyday life, skateboarding abolishes this idea of a playground reserved exclusively for play and games. It also relativizes the idea of play and the game as circumscribed by precise and pre-determined times. It should never be forgotten that the skateboard is before anything a mode of transportation: one can use one's skateboard to go grocery shopping or skate either to school or to the university. These small trips intersect between so many indeterminate zones inherent either to the time of everyday life or play, and with an indeterminacy that lasts as long as it takes to decide whether or not one wants to cut school, skate stairs outside the grocery store, or go in and do one's shopping.

9 When I write "young adult," I am not thinking of teenagers, but rather of two generations of skaters between the ages of 20 and 40. The gap between the ages of the youngest and oldest skaters broadens as skateboarding itself ages.

10 *Le Jardin des planches*, 1977. A documentary by Monique Barrières, 6 min., 15 sec., 35 mm color, cinematography Paul Bonis, produced by Téléma.

11 Jacques Carroux, "Le skate sauvage," *Esprit*, October, 1978.

Skateboarding shares its playing space with those who do not skate, which is to say, those who do not play. This is one of its more salient characteristics. It is not without an impact on our everyday life, and it is often reproached for just this permeability. Skateboarding leaves traces of paint behind, it erodes and sometimes even breaks stone benches and concrete curbs. It is undeniable that skateboarding is an accelerator of entropy. As far as all this is concerned, one thing that must be understood is that skateboarding is never an act of micro-terrorism. The skater does not destroy in order to enrage the local resident, nor does he make noise to exasperate passersby. The noise, the traces and marks are the results of an activity that did not necessarily expect to produce them; it is rather part of the condition of the skater's enjoyment. An enjoyment rather difficult to share, I admit, and one which ultimately consists of testing and playing with the resistance of materials. A skateboard is composed of wood (the deck), polyurethane (the wheels) and aluminum (trucks, which is to say the axles that hold the wheels). Depending on the trick, the skater slides and grinds on a variety of surfaces ranging from benches (the wood), stone (another bench, a single stair), metal (a handrail, a foot traffic barrier, etc), concrete (ledges, Jersey barriers) and so on. Skateboarding seeks to combine, explore and master these different kinds of contact with the urban envirronnement. It is a question of understanding these materials and forms by submitting them to untried physics experiments.[12]

In fact, if skaters are known to modify the spaces and urban objects that they appropriate, they do so rarely. On the square d'Assas in Nîmes, for example, conceived by the artist Martial Raysse, one could notably see stone benches worn down by the skaters who had modified and restored them by adapting metal siding to them. In a public square in Lyon, skaters installed a new handrail, which by virtue of being square and slightly lower than usual, was more suited to their needs.[13] But more so than the skaters, it is usually the cities themselves which modify certain spaces in order to render them "unskatable." In this sense, Montpellier

[12] This is not without recalling a whole aspect of sculpture from the '60s and '70s in which artists engaged in the same kind of experiments with their tools and materials: it would suffice to consider the interactive work of Carl Andre or Richard Serra's many ways of making sculpture. It was a question of making a sculpture whose defining characteristic was the physical experience of the artist and/or the viewer.

is an exemplary city: the municipality chiseled notches every 50 centimeters on all the marble or concrete benches potentially usable by skaters.[14] Bars, at first glance virtually useless, had been installed in front of certain gaps or sets of stairs in order to prevent the possibility of ollies of any sort. If anything, one cannot reproach the city of Montpellier for misunderstanding the mechanics of an activity that it was so successful at eradicating.

When all is said and done, in order to play in the street, teenage and young adult skaters are obliged to take recourse in the same techniques as children. They invent new rules and new stakes, which contribute to the way we negotiate the spaces we inhabit daily.

CATEGORIES, MOTIVES AND RULES

Of the four categories conceived by Caillois, only two (*agôn* and *ilinx*) could be said to characterize the activity of skateboarding. Skateboarding obviously has nothing to do with games of chance (*alea*).[15] The factor of chance, however, is not entirely absent given that the skater appropriates a terrain conceived for another use: his enjoyment is often the fruit of an architect or an urbanist unconscious of having engendered such happiness. Like all sports activities, skateboarding possesses the potential to become a spectacle. But this is not necessarily why it is a form of mimicry, the category presupposed by make believe, the mask and décor.[16] Of course, one could have elected to study the "costumes" and

---

[13] Since the initial publication of this text, and subsequent examples of the DIY skatepark Burnside in Portland, Oregon, and as well as Pontus Alvs spots in Malmö, Sweden, skaters have begun to modify certain spaces of the city with concrete. The development of such spots would require a study specific to this phenomenon; the most prominent examples are cited in "A Day With No Waves."

[14] This is notably the case in Antigone, a residential neighborhood conceived by Ricardo Bofill. I would be very curious to have the opinion of the architect himself: would he rather have the notches or the traces and marks left by the skaters?
Over the course of the past few years, such anti-skateboarding accoutrements have become more and more a part of the urban landscape.

[15] *Alea* (in Latin, a game of dice) is the category reserved for games of chance, "In contrast to *agôn*, *alea* negates work, patience, experience and qualifications [...]. *Alea* is total disgrace or absolute favor." (pg. 17) If the spirit of the *agôn* is linked to free choice, the player of *alea* is totally passive and entirely dependent on the whims of destiny.

[16] The category of *mimicry* is predicated upon the fact the subject "makes believe or makes others believe that he is someone other than himself." (pg. 19) The world of *mimicry* is that of the mask and décor, of the game and the stage, that of representation and the illusion of he who, "for a given time [...] is asked to believe in himself as more real than reality itself." (pg. 23).

poses of skaters. Skateboarding is an aesthetic activity on several levels. The demanding skater does not only work to master a given trick, but works also on his style, in terms of its beauty and grace. The aesthetics of movement is coupled with that of the skater himself; the way of being and doing are intimately linked, sometimes to the point of excess.

Agôn (which in Greek means war, combat) is the category of play which represents the spirit of competition. It presupposes the effort, the assiduity, and the will to vanquish, as well as discipline and perseverance. From which it follows that: "*Agôn* is a vindication of personal responsibility." (pg 18) Caillois specifies that the spirit of *agôn* can also be found outside of the game, or at the limit of the game, in the duel or the tournament, for example. But competition is not always of the order of the duel, and Caillois remarks the difference between "legitimately competitive games and sports," and "feats of prowess," among which he classifies "hunting, mountain climbing, crossword puzzles, chess problems, etc., in which champions, without directly confronting each other, are involved in ceaseless and diffuse competition." (pg 17)

Whether evocative of the world of childhood or high flying acrobatics, the games designated under the rubric *ilinx* (a Greek noun for "whirlpool," one of its derivatives *ilingos* describes vertigo) are linked to the search for vertigo and thrills. These games "include [...] those which are based on the pursuit of vertigo and which consist of an attempt to momentarily destroy the stability of perception and inflict a kind of voluptuous panic upon an otherwise lucid mind. In all cases, it is a question of surrendering to a kind of spasm, seizure or shock which destroys reality with sovereign brusqueness." (pg 23) Merry-go-rounds, toboggans, swings, as well as racing down slopes and screaming at the top of one's lungs, all these forms of play can be gathered into the *ilinx* category. Beyond childhood, adults are able to seek these kinds of sensations in diverse forms linked to speed. Caillois gives the examples of skiing or motorcycle riding, as well as amusement parks with their "vertigo machines." Among the *ilinx* forms of play, we experience the passage from fear to pleasure.

Within these categories, Caillois distinguishes the antagonistic poles between which all the ways of playing can be located. On one side, we have *paidia*, the "motive power" in every anarchic, exuberant, turbulent and improvised form of play. On the other, there is *ludus*, that which comes to bind the anarchic nature of *paidia*, "with arbitrary, imperative, and purposely tedious conventions." (pg 13)

Paidia is the original and indispensable motivating power for play or the game. *Ludus* establishes rules, limits and complicates the game by codifying in significant, arbitrary advances the initial impulse. It renders the game more difficult, multiplies its facets by incorporating certain constraints; the more numerous and complex the obstacles and difficulties of the game, the greater its value. *Ludus* presupposes effort, patience, skill and ingenuity. It is "complementary to and a refinement of *paidia*, which it disciplines and enriches." (pg 29) Its development, which is that of the rule, establishes a stable order, "a tacit legislation in a lawless universe." Thus is the game a way of countering the arbitrariness which governs the world, and as such generates a sense of temporary control by investing reality with a meaning that otherwise escapes us. To play is to also create a world to one's own measure.

Skateboarding initially belongs to the category of *agôn*, even if it seems to distance itself from it, like all the other disciplines designated "prowesses," "in which champions, without directly confronting each other, are involved in ceaseless and diffuse competition." [17] (pg 17) As in any activity of prowess, the player is firstly his own adversary. By essence, skateboarding is an individual game, a solitary activity. However the goal of solitary practice leads undeniably to a group activity, as skateboarding depends largely upon the tacit competition that is emulation.

The difficulties that the skater seeks to resolve are double. They implicate his relationship to the diversity of spaces as much as skateboarding itself. A board is not simply a vehicle, it is also a kind of juggling tool. As a vehicle, it allows for a certain relationship of the body with the surrounding space where the skater chooses his obstacles. This is the common dominator of "extreme sports." But in a more "reflexive" practice, the tool of the skateboard becomes its own, unique obstacle: the skater functions like a juggler, submitting his skateboard to a series of various complex tricks, consisting above all of differing kinds of gyrations. Here,

---

17 Among which Caillois mentions chess as well as rock climbing.

the only thing that counts is the skater's relationship to the tool, as space is not used except in its most basic sense: as a flat, smooth plane.[18] Skateboarding proceeds from a tripartite compound of body-tool-space:

1. In the body-space relationship in which the skateboard is the intermediary (skateboard as a vehicle), space is the obstacle (space or an element within the space). For example: to ollie over a fire hydrant or a set of stairs, slide on a bench or down a handrail.

2. In the body-skateboard relationship (skateboard as a tool) in which the space is the intermediary (in its most basic sense) and the skateboard is obstacle. For example: the skateboard enacts a flip.

3. Mixing together the first two schemas, a relationship of the body to space means the use of the skateboard both as a tool and a vehicle: the obstacle is twofold, it is the space + the skateboard. For example: to ollie over an obstacle while the board itself enacts a flip.

The specificity of skateboarding is very simple. It is that which allows for a temporary lack of union between the tool-body couple, which other extreme sports allow at most in a very limited measure. This invests the vehicle with the possibility of moving independently of the body. As with juggling, the success of a given maneuver depends on the synchronization between the movements of the body and the tool [19] (of the tool-vehicle in the case of the skater).

Skateboarding is, without a doubt, no stranger to sensations of vertigo and the intoxication of speed, exhibiting a certain taste for risk. It nevertheless structures and frames vertigo. The "vertigo" of skateboarding is not a complete loss of the points of reference which link a skater to reality. If skateboarding fits into the category of *ilinx*, we shouldn't forget to specify that it is with a maximum *ludus*. Therefore, alongside gymnastics and high flying acrobatics, which, according to Caillois, are nothing more than

---

18 This essentially reflexive practice is what was known in the '70s and '80s as freestyle, that form of skateboarding that is the closest to dancing and juggling. From freestyle, which disappeared as a form at the beginning of the '90s, was born a whole new genre of skating, known as "flat skating." Much more dynamic than freestyle, which tends to remain in same place, flat skating eventually phased out any tricks explicitly reminiscent of gymnastics.

19 A successful trick adheres to the following schema: beginning, "unity," trick "disunity" reception, "re-unification."

extensions of those games initially played as a child, they have become structured to the point of refinement to its most extreme point by *ludus*. In the same *ilinx* column (see the annex) of its summary table, Caillois situates children's games such as the slide, the merry go round, screaming at the top of one's lungs, or running at full speed down a hill, as close as possible to the *paidia* pole. While at the other end can be found skiing, rock climbing and high flying acrobatics.

This gradation of the "slide" to the "sliding" allows us to rethink skateboarding under a new light of early childhood games. I don't think it would be an act of over-interpretation to present skateboarding as an amalgam of tastes and "vertiginous prowesses" akin to those of a child: a fascination for the wheel (a toy car with pedals), the enjoyment of speed (the toboggan, the swing [20]), high, long and degree jumps [21] (the general desire to be weightless), rapid spins, [22] and of course, the act of sliding down handrails, which remains one of the most spectacular (re)inventions of skateboarding. [23] Skateboarding is therefore the world of codified infantile prowess, structured in a way so as to always allow for free expression of a certain child-like "anarchy." And I do not find it strange to think that skateboarding, by virtue of the complexity of its maneuvers and the possibility of exploiting the urban space which surrounds us, gives the teenager the ability to affirm his identity at an age when he often has the feeling that everything is beyond his control. It is a tool that allows one to fulfill, in a concrete form, a need for disorder, even destruction, which is nevertheless accompanied by the creation of a new order of a more personal nature. Of the slide and other similar children's games, and the vertigo they proffer, Caillois says, "[it] is readily linked to the desire for disorder and destruction, a drive which is normally

---

[20] The structure of one and the pendulous movement of the other do not fail to recall the form and use of skateboards ramps (half-pipes).

[21] I remember playing alone as a child on a set of stairs, jumping from the first stair to the ground, then the second, the third, etc. in order to test myself, but even more so in a contest with one or more friends in order to test our abilities and our courage.

[22] Here, one is reminded of the multiple rotations executed by freestylers in the '70s and '80s as well as of ramp tricks whose names correspond to the degrees of rotation: from the 360 (a complete turn) to 900 (two and a half turns), in between which, both historically and literally, can be found the famous McTwist (a complete turn and a half involved a kind of partially front flip).

[23] The first board slides down hand rails date to 1987. They are generally attributed to street skating pioneers: Natas Kaupas and Mark Gonzales.

repressed." (pg 24). The practice of skateboarding, especially during the teenage years, seems to me to constantly oscillate between the mastery of self and a sense of excess.

Skateboarding is an activity that is much more codified than it is governed by rules. It's even possible to consider almost all "extreme sports" as a more or less explicit critique of rules. Skateboarding is above all an individual game where the acquisition of gestures, of tricks (which are combined) allows one to augment the potential of the terrain. Of course, very few skaters invent new tricks, but anyone can discover a new terrain, a new obstacle, and adapt thereupon one's repertoire of tricks while seeking to expand that repertoire. The affirmation of identity and personal recognition are not only measured by the difficulty of the maneuver. The choice of terrain is also expressive: to skate is also to see, to know how to look and to adapt.

THE FORBIDDEN CONJUNCTION: AGON-ILINX

The theory of the conjunction between different categories of games marks a turn in Caillois' book. This is the point at which Caillois attempts to shift from a sociology of play and games, to a sociology whose point of departure is play and games. Of all the possible conjunctions—competition-chance (*agôn-alea*), competition-simulation (*agôn-mimicry*), competition-vertigo (*agôn-ilinx*), chance-simulation (*alea-mimicry*), chance-vertigo (*alea-ilinx*), simulation-vertigo (*mimicry-ilinx*)—two seem to him essential, two are viable, and two, finally, are incompatible. Caillois does not take into consideration tripartite compositions, which, according to him, are more often than not occasional juxtapositions.

At this point in my reading of *Man, Play and Games*, I had no doubt that skateboarding, as well as the majority of "extreme sports" corresponded to the *agôn-ilinx* conjunction, in which competition is associated with vertigo. However, a page later, Caillois classifies this binary as among the two forbidden conjunctions. The reason for this is simple and logical: "The paralysis it [vertigo] provokes, like the blind fury it causes in other cases, is a strict negation of controlled effort." (pg 72)

If Caillois's system in its entirety cannot really be used to specifically describe skateboarding, it is nevertheless worth pausing to consider the subject for a moment, before going further on in the study of the forbidden conjunction.

The second incompatible coupling is the one which unites chance and simulation (*alea-mimicry*): "Alea presupposes full and total abandon to the whims of chance, submission to which is incompatible with disguise or subterfuge. Otherwise, one enters the domain of magic, the object of which is to coerce destiny." (pg. 73) Contingent conjunctions are chance coupled with vertigo (*alea-ilinx*), which corresponds to the "vertigo of the player," as well as the pair, competition-simulation (*agôn-mimicry*), it being understood that all competition is spectacular, in the sense of being a spectacle.

The fundamental conjunctions therefore are competition-chance (*agôn-alea*) and simulation-vertigo (*mimicry-ilinx*), chance and competition representing two complementary aspects of the same attitude vis-à-vis the world. This attitude is that of the rule where all is defined beforehand; for Caillois, this coupling is characteristic of civilization. Chance and competition, "create law [societies], i.e., a fixed, abstract, and coherent code." (pg. 126). The society of this fundamental conjunction is, according to the author's expression, that of "merit and birth right." In order to balance the fortuity of birth (or produce a stronger illusion of the equality of the law), our societies had the idea of games of chance, the lottery. But on the side of merit as much as on the side of chance, there are many calls for a select elite, and man is obliged to take recourse in "delegation" or to use a psychoanalytical term, "projection." The common man is granted access to what he considers extraordinary through a star, a singer, an athlete or a movie star.

The world that corresponds to the second fundamental conjunction, *mimicry* and *ilinx*, is that of the mask and the trance, of such practices as shamanism and voodoo. They are linked to the sphere of the sacred in which can be remarked a "combination of [...] ecstasy and simulation." (pg. 93) In Roger Caillois' system this conjunction defines so-called primitive cultures.

It is useful to remember that *Man, Play and Games* was published in the middle of the '50s and that Caillois revised and completed the work ten years later. Even if it had been possible for him to include skiing in this study (and even without considering the ins and outs of this sport), in the contexte of France in the 1950s he couldn't have considered surfing, because it was only just emerging at that time in the United States (and only came to France a little later by way of Biarritz). The first wave of skateboarding in the middle of the '60s would arrive in France in a rather attenuated form. [24] It would be necessary to wait another ten years before certain people, such as Jacques Carroux (and in a very isolated mode [25]) would be able to pick up on the stakes of such an activity. In order to find the commencement of a theory for extreme sports, [26] one has to wait for chapter IX, "Revivals in the Modern World." Our civilized world would then be characterized by the *agôn-alea* conjunction. But given that the return of the repressed is inevitable, we are bound to witness, in the modern world, the revival of *mimicry* and *ilinx*. I will leave *mimicry* aside in order to concentrate exclusively on *ilinx*. Caillois explains that the return of vertigo happens by way of the funfair (let's say today's amusement or theme parks) and high flying acrobatics (which we add while also noting that within the forms referred to in the book, spectacles of stuntmen are no longer really contemporary). It is necessary to return to this feeling of vertigo, to attempt to better describe it, to return to certain characteristics of the autonomous category of *ilinx* via the fun park or the circus.

In fun parks, teenagers and adults try to regain the feeling of an original vertigo, that which brings them back, as closely as possible, to the experience of their toys as children (therefore, as close as possible to *paidia*, of the total loss of control). In order to adapt the merry-go-round, the swing, the toboggan to the measure of an adult, and create a game in which a responsible adult can relinquish any sense of responsibility, industrial society con-

[24] For more on this subject, see Jean Barral's 1966 documentary, *Le Surf au Trocadero*, 5 min, 51 sec, black and white, 16mm, produced by ORTF, series Dim dam dom, produced by Daisy de Galant.
[25] I have never seen another article by the writer on this subject. And this article was originally featured in an issue of the magazine *Esprit* dedicated to the research of Michel de Certeau on the culture of the ordinary. Carroux's article was part of a collection of three texts by different writers, who address the return to the city after the hippy utopias by way of rock music (punk and new wave) and skateboarding. I will probably explore in a future text the parallels between development of skateboarding and punk music, even of early skateboarding as "punk sport."
[26] In the sense of how they are analyzed by the likes of, most notably, David le Breton in certain articles and then in longer texts in which the notion of risk is the common denominator, "Passions du risque" in 1991, or more recently in "Conduites à risque," 2002, Presses universitaires de France, coll. "Quadrige," Paris, 2002.

structed enormous "vertigo machines." "In order to give this kind of sensation the intensity and brutality capable of shocking adults, powerful machines have had to be invented. Thus it is not surprising that the Industrial Revolution had to take place before vertigo could really become a kind of game." (pg 25) Every kind of vertiginous spinning wheel marks the return to childhood. On such mechanisms, one is shaken, thrown about, flipped over, hurled at great speeds forward and just as suddenly brought to a halt, in a word: assisted. It is a question of vertigo of consumption, or, as Caillois so beautifully puts it, the individual becomes "the toy of the toy." The relationship between the toy and the subject is inverted, but this is not the only reversal remarked by the writer. The second reversal takes place by virtue of a fundamental principle of civilized societies, "delegation" and its correlative, "projection": "The spectators are made to pay for the privilege of calmly observing from a high balcony the terrors of the co-operating or surprised victims, exposed to fearful forces or strange caprices."[27] (pg 26) It is a phenomenon of vicarious vertigo experienced by those watching the spinning wheel rides.

We should now count among this duality, which allows us to establish a scale of safety among such thrill-seeking:
— the vertiginous spectacle of the other,
— assisted vertigo,
— controlled vertigo.

The domain of controlled vertigo generally belongs to acrobats and stuntmen, but no less to skaters and adepts of extreme sports. This controlled vertigo, especially in the world of spectacle as entertainment (but we shall see that extreme sports can be addressed only from this angle) only makes sense in relationship to the first category, that which groups together all thrill-seeking feelings through an intermediary. Before the spectacle of assisted vertigo, the real risk is too slight for the process of projection to function without a kind of collective frenzy, likewise organized (by the visual and auditory density of the separated spaces which constitute fun parks).

---

[27] Caillois continues: "It would be rash to draw very precise conclusions on the subject of this curious and cruel assignment of roles. This last is not characteristic of a kind of game, such as is found in boxing, wrestling, and gladiatorial combat." (pg. 26) Caillois who doesn't want to "draw very precise conclusions" from this phenomenon, draws none; he doesn't revisit the subject.

THE FORBIDDEN CONJUNCTION

The acrobat plays with heights, with a kind of void. By dominating his fear, he transforms it into a kind of ally. He seeks to give us the impression that the void no longer exists for him. But this void which no longer exists for him must exist for the viewer. This is the condition for vicarious vertigo. If the viewer grows too used to the supple gesture of the acrobat, the latter simulates a fall in order to renew the process of projection. The circus, like the fun park, is a place separated from the everyday. Acrobats use a whole host of accessories: mats, trapezes, ropes and nets. From time to time, the tightrope walker can stretch a rope between two buildings, and thus take a step into our everyday life.

The stuntman assumes the role of the acrobat in the industrial age. His motorcycles, cars, etc., are closer to us than trapezes and nets. But he is still a man of spectacle, of entertainment, and the stuntman uses a kind of etiquette meant to liken him to the popular image of the super-hero (the modern demi-God). This factor marks the distance that separates him from the public (common mortals). He is not yet the ordinary anti-hero expected by a certain generation. The stuntman has simply replaced the props and tools of the acrobat. The human canonball competed for a time with the timeless tamer of savage animals.

In 1995, the cable channel ESPN organized the first X-Games, a large sports competition featuring skateboarding, rollerblading and BMX contests in a giant skatepark especially constructed for the occasion. This televised program, which was destined for a broad audience, emphasized the "dramatic" side of skateboarding. Undeniably, the contemporary image of skaters circulated by the famous X-Games is based on that of American stuntmen,[28] who have given up their glitzy lifestyle in order to create the illusion of everyday life among Hollywood's cinematic spectacles. But the real dominion of the everyday skater-stuntman is not the skatepark or extreme games, it is the street: ordinary space promoted to the terrain of the extreme game. It seems to me, and cinema tends to confirm this, that a stunt has more of an impact if it seems to take place in the everyday world. The exoticism of the stunt of the "exotic" exploit may make one dream, but it remains distant from us (therefore far from the possibility of identification). Contrary to the skier or surfer, the skater does not aid in the propagation of a myth of elsewhere, of a possible return to nature, which is implicit in almost all extreme sports. If there is any kind of communion—and why shouldn't there be?—it is with an asphalt and concrete that is often decried. [29] It cannot be doubted that urban stunts are more directly admired by teenagers in cities. Such stunts put into play, in the most accessible way, the question of one's relationship to space, of the self as an element of the general social body. The thrill of risk sought by skaters is made all the more remarkable by virtue of the fact that it happens in such a seemingly secure and safe place. As such, skaters help forge a new myth of the everyday stuntman. If, in the case of skateboarding, the process of projection functions so well, it is because he who watches knows and understands the obstacles, and physically and stylistically recognizes himself in the model of projection.

In an activity where the body is not protected by a metal armature, the dexterity of the player also becomes his armature. In my opinion, the skater only enjoys a given thrill retrospectively, once the uncomfortable position he has put himself in has

[28] Even if the image of the skater-stuntman is far from being embraced by all professional skaters, many of whom still boycott the X-Games, certain of them (like Duane Peters, Danny Way and Jamie Thomas) do not seek to conceal their admiration for the celebrated stuntman Evel Knievel, who, on a motorcycle, jumped over 36 cars. Since the middle of the '90s, we have seen photos and footage of skaters (Jeremy Wray, Tony Hawk, Daewon Song, etc.) ollieing from one rooftop to another. At the time of the composition of this text, Danny Way holds the world record for the longest air on a ramp, which is structurally reminiscent of the one used by Evel Knievel for making his jumps. At the end of the '70s, Duane Peters and Kent Senatore pulled off a complete rotation of a tube (or more precisely, a partially enclosed càpsule). Thirty years later, Tony Hawk, Bob Burnquist and others, renew the feat with the Loop, a feature of a wooden skatepark which consists of a closed loop or tube. It has already been a few years since handrails have come to dominate skate videos. Boardslides and grinds down handrails become more and more complex, the handrails themselves, longer and longer. The physical risks have increased, and the consequent falls or "slams" more and more spectacular. It is not unusual that videos show footage of various fractures and serious injuries.

[29] It is necessary to write a completely different text on the question of re-evaluating the urban landscape. This minor history would contain the history of the Z-Boys (the teenagers—in part—who invented modern skateboarding and whose story is related by Stacy Peralta and Craig Stecyck's documentary, *Dogtown and Z-Boys*), punk counterculture and the concept of "artialisation" theorized by Alain Roger, which consists of vouchsafing a given landscape a kind of artistic status, e.g., Cézanne's Mont Saint Victoire. One could even imagine a detour in the sublime landscape: mountains, ocean, desert; showing how extreme sports have appropriated the first two, leaving the desert to such mechanical sports as the Paris-Dakar car race. Using this model, it would be a question of showing how the big city is a new, sublime landscape, which both frightens and fascinates, and how certain activities attempt to "commune" with it, or at least master, through action and détournement, this leviathan. The idea would be to propose a continuum of concrete-tar as a fifth element, with the Belgian artist Wim Delvoye's wooden-cement truck as its icon.

been overcome. He cannot enjoy vertigo except through mastery of the thrill. Caillois would undoubtedly say that he cancels it out, but I don't think so. On the contrary, each "canceled" thrill inevitably represents the challenge of another which will follow, more vertiginous than the one which preceded it. The objective of *ludus* is to complicate the activity while increasing the level of vertigo. Let us use an example with which many skaters will be familiar: one learns to simply ollie down a set of three stairs, which constitutes the first thrill. Once that is mastered, one complicates things and ollies down the same set of stairs, but turns 180 degrees while doing so, then tries a kick flip, etc., each new difficulty being the occasion of a new thrill. Eventually, once one's repertoire of tricks has been exhausted, one graduates to a set of stairs with four steps.

This idea of vertigo goes quite well, in our spectacular society, with the development of various medias, and the proliferation of visual recording mechanisms. Everything seems capable of being recorded, seen, shown, whence the progressive extinction of the unseen gesture, the complete loss. Few either professional or amateur skaters attempt tricks without being filmed by a digital camera. Even if skateboarding contests exist, the real contest takes place among videos. Most contests are organized on artificial terrains. Like all predominantly aesthetic disciplines (gymnastics, figure skating, etc.), judgement is above all qualitative. Quantitative competitions in skateboarding such as those that involve speed, slalom, high jump, etc are nowadays rather rare. Where such challenges persist (high air contest, ollie contest), it is often in the margin of qualitative contests, which are judged in terms of consecutive series of tricks, style, how space is used, etc. Many skaters, especially those who believe that the street is the only viable terrain, refuse to compete in contests. Technology gives them a new form of *agôn*, which is even more indirect. In skate videos, the aesthetic sense is pushed to its breaking point; every aspect is geared toward investing each skater with a particular tonality. The video footage itself consists of a kind of "best of" of each skater, the tricks and spots are edited into montage, shown one after another, without seeking to create any kind of temporal or spatial unity, or abiding by any code aside from rhythm and aesthetics. There is no narrative. In some cases, however, a narrative is interposed between parts of different skaters. [30] The music is supposed to resonate with the style of the skater: his personal style (haircut, clothes), the different types of terrain he skates (or those he is particularly fond of), his repertoire of tricks and the way as well as the sequence in which he executes them. The way he films and shows his parts can be seen as an integral aspect of his aesthetic (clean, punk, or lo-fi) and invest a given company with his identity.

The skater's sense of thrill seems to have become inseparable from the awareness he has of being watched, therefore, of being able to produce thrills. To dominate vertigo is to likewise transmit that experience to others, those physically present as well as who might see it on a screen. This mechanism of transmitting vertigo is a new form parallel to diffuse competition.

---

30 See for example *The Search for Animal Chin*, Powell Peralta, 1987; *Streets on Fire*, Santa Cruz, 1989; *Video Days*, Blind, 1991; Mouse, Girl, 1996, etc.

EPILOGUE

Caillois did not foresee the secularization of big tent acrobatics. He did not anticipate acrobatics as one of the future possibilities of street games. The return of the *ilinx* in civilization, which is to say, in a society governed by laws, fixed codes and coherence (characterized by the couple *agôn-alea*) implies the resurgence of a primitive element.

The "primitive" element is a certain form of initiatory rite, which David le Breton, in his study of extreme sports and risk-prone activities, qualifies as a "trial by ordeal rite." The trial by ordeal is a "judiciary right inscribed in a cultural system that appeals to god or several gods to regulate humankind." [31] It is a question of confronting someone with death in order to know if he deserves to live. But the contemporary trial by ordeal for Le Breton is a figure of a given individual's unconscious, it becomes "an intimate solicitation, an oracular rite with a strictly personal value." [32] By running the risk of death or seriously wounding oneself, while providing oneself with the opportunity to opt out at any time, the individual proves the value of his existence. "The modern passion for risks is rooted in a context troubled by a crisis of meaning, of a discomfort with individual and collective identities." [33] Thanks to a lack of cultural limits, the adepts of vertigo-risks seek physical limits in activities where "reality tends to replace the symbolic." [34]

These activities proliferated at the end of the '70s, parallel to the rise of punk music, which is to say, in reaction against hippy dreams. Contrary to a thinking that preached a return to nature, to dreaming and transcendence, punk is the city, concrete, immanence. The weight of the everyday becomes the subject and the very material of the music. In the same way, skateboarding is a reconquest of urban space. Among an architecture conceived not for the citizen, but for the consumer, which is to say, in cities where the notion of public space is replaced by that of commercial space, skaters attempt to reconnect with a use of the city; the skater can then be perceived as a producer of public space [35] in the heart of commercial space.

---

[31] David Le Breton, *Conduites à risque*, op. cit., p. 110. Citation translated by Chris Sharp.
[32] Ibid.
[33] David Le Breton, "Le fil de rasoir," in *Exposé #2*, Pertes d'Inscription, Orléans, 1995. Pg. 117. Citation translated by Chris Sharp.
[34] Ibid., pg. 118.

As Iain Borden puts it in his remarkable book, *Skateboarding, Space and the City*, the objects of the everyday urban world are functional and highly programmed. They are all the vectors of a message; they speak a unilateral, authoritarian language, which conditions us and with which we cannot communicate.[36] The city is full of ideas, culture, memory, financial exchanges, information and ideologies. Skaters spontaneously suspend the power implicit in each building, space and object of urban furniture, reducing the city to its essence, a play of materials put into form.[37] "A painting" wrote Maurice Denis in his article 'Definition of Neo-Traditionalism, "before being a battle horse, a nude woman or whatever anecdote is essentially a flat surface covered with colors and a certain order." Intuitively, and through action, skateboarding expresses a similar idea of the city.

In an often heavy and oppressive reality, the skater could be the figure of lightness as expressed by Italo Calvino.[38] A contemporary Perseus, the skater inserts between himself and the Medusa of the world, seven fine plys of laminated oak mounted on a wheels. The skateboard, which allows one to slide along the surface of things, is at once a pair of winged shoes and a shield-mirror. In another one of Calvino's parables, he uses a story from *The Decameron* wherein Boccaccio describes how the poet Guido Cavalcanti, supporting himself on a tomb, escaped his bellicose assailants in a single bound. The skater is also Cavalcanti.

A retreat? A flight? Perhaps when all is said and done, but what matter the flight, if skateboarding and the imagery it generates are a way of re-evaluating urban space, the tar-concrete continuum.

When parents show sand to their child, he or she looks at the nearby concrete. Enjoying the leisure of the beach is a habit that has not always been natural. But to enjoy the leisure of concrete is

---

35 On this subject, see the essay by the ex-professional skater Ocean Howell, *The Poetics of Security: Skateboarding, Urban Design, and the New Public Space*, 2001 (available on the internet). The issue of the skater as a producer of public space is addressed in "The Question Is Which is To Be The Master?" My idea however is that skateboarding does not create public space, but rather helps to question it.

36 For more information on the subject, see Iain Borden's comprehensive, *Skateboarding, Space and the City*, Berg, Oxford, 2001, p. 191.
37 Iain Borden, ibid., pg. 213
38 Italo Calvino, *Six Memos for the Next Millennium*,The Charles Eliot Norton Lectures 1985-86. Vintage International, New York. 1993

a challenge. To transform "here" into an elsewhere, to make everyday space that of play and pleasure is the real activity of the skater. But we will never be easily rid of a "geographical elsewhere," and nothing will ever prevent the skater, on his small city square, from dreaming of Bercy (Paris), the Macba steps (Barcelona) or Pier 7 in San Francisco. After all, while on vacation in La Grande-Motte, it is not forbidden to dream of Costa Rica's beaches.

THE QUESTION IS WHICH IS TO BE MASTER

Francesco Finizio's sculpture *Silver Surfers* (2005) consists of a little pile of skateboard decks partially burned in a campfire. That piece always reminds me of the anachronistic, nay, archaic character of a skateboard deck: seven thin layers of maple cross laminated together.

Following the advice of his wood-worker father, Willie Winkel, a young Canadian skater, conceives the first seven-ply maple skateboard deck in 1976. This new process quickly replaces decks made out of oak, various kinds of plastic, fiberglass, aluminum and other compounds. Since then, things haven't changed at all. A handful of diehard fanatics of innovation have provided us with a few minor discoveries, most of which only go on to prove the contrary: that nothing is better than maple.

In one of the essays featured in his famous collection, *Mythologies,* from the mid-1950s, Roland Barthes laments the disappearance of wooden toys, which have been replaced by figurative metal and plastic toys (from little cars to dolls, not to mention tea sets and revolvers of every kind). Although significantly discredited by the invention of Lego, Barthes' analysis remains germane and could easily be used to describe the relationship a skater has with the forms that surround him or her. The toys that Barthes disparages "always mean something, and this something is always entirely socialized, constituted by the myths or the techniques of modern adult life."[1] According to Barthes, these toys prepare the child to immediately accept the adult world with its values, from war to housekeeping. But what Barthes reproaches them for above all is how they socialize a child as owner-user and never as creator: "Faced with this world of faithful and complicated objects, the child [...] does not invent the world, he uses it: There are prepared for him actions without adventure, without wonder, without joy. He is turned into a little stay-at-home householder who does not even have to invent the mainsprings of adult causality; they are supplied to him ready-made: he has only to help himself, he is never allowed to discover anything from start to finish."[2] Building blocks, and later, Lego (in their most abstract version) implicate the child in a demiurgical activity, in which the meaning, use of, and overall aggregate form of these elements is determined by the child alone.

The objects and spaces from our everyday life are no less subject to this schema; they are conceived for a specific use, determining our gestures and our movements. Like laws, urbanism and its codes are from the outset an attempt to organize the city in hopes of addressing a genuine problem: How can we live together on healthy and equal terms? Nevertheless, architecture and urbanism both often seem to be repressive (however slight that repression might be) with regards to freedom. The notion of commercial space tends more and more to systematically replace public space. In an architecture conceived not for the citizen, but for the consumer, skaters ask the question: What do we do with our cities? As Iain Borden remarks in his book *Skateboarding, Space and the City*, everyday urban objects are functional and highly programmed.[3] They are all vectors of a message. They speak an

---

[1] Roland Barthes, *Mythologies*. Trans., Annette Lavers (New York: Hill and Wang, 1972), pg 53
[2] *Ibid.* pg 54
[3] Iain Borden, *Skateboarding, Space and the City* (Oxford: Berg Publishers, 2001). See notably the two chapters "Urban Composition" and "Performing the City."

authoritarian, unilateral language, which conditions us and with which it is impossible to communicate. The activity of the skaters tends to spontaneously suspend the implicit power in each building, space, object or piece of urban furniture; skaters reduce the city to its essence, a game-like collection of materials put into form. By disengaging it from its intended use and depriving architecture of its meaning, skateboarding becomes a way to appropriate the city, or, to use Barthes' vocabulary, becomes a way to exist as a "creator" rather than as a simple "user."

In *Through the Looking-Glass*, Humpty Dumpty says to Alice:
"When *I* use a word, [...] it means just what I choose it to mean—neither more nor less."
"The question [responds Alice] is whether you *can* make words mean so many different things."
"The question is," said Humpty Dumpty, "which is to be master—that's all."[4]

Skaters invent new uses for certain patches of the urban fabric of cities. In the spirit of Humpty Dumpty, non-English speakers (around the world) often choose to use the words like curb, ledge or handrail as opposed to their counterparts in their own languages. But these words are more than simple English, they designate new objects, a parallel reality where the reasons to be a curb or handrail are something else entirely. Through action, skaters modify the meaning as well as the history of the spaces they appropriate. These words crystallize this modification: a handrail is only a handrail as it used by a skater.

In his remarkable essay *The Poetics of Security*,[5] Ocean Howell maintains that skaters rectify the commercial logic of certain spaces, and thus become producers of public spaces. In my opinion, skateboarding, which very effectively asks the question of how to redefine public space, does not as effectively answer it. Skaters are not producers of public spaces in the sense that they open up spaces to other practices. More often than not, skaters end up annexing a space rather than sharing it. What is more, it is

4 Lewis Carroll, *Through the Looking Glass* (London: Penguin Classics, 1998), Chapter 6 "Humpty Dumpty"

5 Ocean Howell, "The Poetics of Security: Skateboarding, Urban Design, and the New Public Space," *Urban Action Journal*, 2001

not so much skaters who can't bear others, but others who often find the fact of being around skateboarding rather difficult and invasive (which is quite legitimate). Skateboarding offers individual, rather than collective, solutions; it is not a civic-minded activity. It is through a sense of play, and thrill-seeking (and all the egotism that inevitably entails) that skaters short-circuit the pre-established use of certain spaces.

In 1978, Jacques Carroux perspicaciously remarked: "Based on what we have seen, the success of skateboarding underlines, at the same that it seeks to remedy, the difficulty of practicing sports in our cities, especially the large ones."[6] While the game or sports are a traditionally separate activity, circumscribed in a particular space and time (Caillois), such protocols do not apply to skateboarding—it imposes itself upon certain spaces shared with pedestrians who are not doing it, and this is one of the main reasons it is often criticized. The architectural degradation caused by skateboarding in certain spaces is undeniable. And yet, skateboarding should not be perceived as a form of vandalism. It is an activity in which enjoyment is more important than any kind of cultural or individual affirmation, and aesthetics are more important than any sense of aggression; the noise, traces and damage caused by skateboarding have never been its motives but rather its simple consequences.

On the model of surfing, it was the large, coastal cities that engendered skateboarding. Today, cities generally consider skateboarding to be a malady that afflicts architecture.[7] The issue of skateboarding must, in my opinion, continue to formulate itself in rather contradictory terms: how can this practice be legally integrated into the heart of the city, without giving up its savage and untamed side? In other words, retain its spirit of dissent?

One thing is certain, the vandalism of skaters is as tangential and indirect as their critique of public space. I do not see why the formula applied to viewing art since Duchamp should not be applied to everyday life: skateboarding is above all that which the observer makes of it.

[6] Jacques Carroux, "Le Skate Sauvage," *Esprit* magazine, October 1978

[7] On this point, please refer again to Ocean Howell's text.

INDEX OF
A CHRONICLE
OF SKATEBOARDING
1779-2009

101, 57, 63
1031, 92
1281, 58
3M, 22
411, 62
5th District, 91
88 Footwear, 78
A Onda Dura, 75
A Skate Park that Glides the Land & Drops Into the Sea, 85
A Team, 68, 74
A Visual Sound, 65
AB 1296 law, 68
Abre los ojos, 66
Acconci, Vito, 75, 85
Acme, 61, 62
Action Now, 36
Adams, Jason, 62, 76, 77
Adams, Jay, 13, 19, 20, 21, 22, 23, 24, 26, 32, 61, 87
Adidas, 61, 68, 78
Agah, Salman, 56, 63, 64, 76
Agent Orange, 42
Aggression, 42
Airwalk, 44, 53, 61, 64, 106
Alai, 92
Alba, Micky "Malba", 31, 33, 37
Alba, Steve "Salba", 31, 33, 37, 50, 94
Albuquerque (ditch), 25
Alfaro, Adam, 76
Alias Distribution, 78
Alien Workshop, 56, 62, 92, 104, 107
All Girls Skate Jam (contest), 70
Alleged Gallery (New York), 70
Allen, Ron, 39, 51
Almost, 87, 105
Alphaville, 17
Alter, Hobie, 14, 15, 16, 17
Alv, Pontus, 79, 83, 88, 99
Alva Skateboards, 27
Alva, Tony, 12, 19, 20, 21, 22, 23, 24, 25, 26, 27, 29, 32, 34, 40, 48, 63, 87
Amenabar, Alejandro, 66
Ameron Plant (full-pipes), 28
Ancell, Kevin, 43
Anderson, Brian, 27, 67, 72, 73
Anderson, Kenny, 106
Andrade, Carlos de, 68
Andrecht, 37
Anti Hero, 74, 81, 105
Antigone, (skatepark), 54
Antiz, 98
Anyway, 57
Appleyard, Mark, 78, 82, 106
Araujo Jr., Rodil de, 68
Archers of Loaf, 67
Are you Alright?, 86
Arguelles, Felix, 44
Armejo, Richard, 38
Atchley, Brent, 78, 81
Ayres, Gregg, 37
B-Side, 65
Bachinsky, Dave, 94

Back to the futur, 43
Bacon, Edmund, 89, 90
Bad Brains, 63
Badgett, Steven et Lynch, 75
Badlands (full-pipe), 19
Bahne Cadillac Internationals, see Del Mar Nationals, 23
Bahne Cadillac, 21, 23
Bahne Skateboard, 20, 21, 23
Bahne, Billy, 23
Bajo, Delia, 76
Baker 3, 91
Baker, 74, 107
Baker, Lacey, 74, 107
Balma, Larry, 40, 41
Baltimore, Megan, 63
Ban This, 54
Barajas, Armando, 55
Barbee, Ray, 50, 56, 61
Barbier, Sal, 56, 57, 64
Barley, Donny, 67
Basquiat, Jean-Michel, 85
Bassett, Zered, 106
Bassins de la tour Eiffel (Paris), 28, 51
Battle at the Berrics (contest), 102, 106
Baudier, Raymond, 33
Baxter Neal, Silas, 103
Bayonne (contest), 30
Beach Boys, 15
Bearer, Danny, 14, 18
Beato, Greg, 73, 87
Beautiful Losers, 85
Behrns, Don, 77
Bellagio Elementary School (Los Angeles, Californie), 21
Bennett Hijacker, 22
Berra, Steve, 60, 102, 103
Berrichons Associés (les), 43, 47, 57
Bertino, Ronnie, 64
Bertlemann, Larry, 22, 25, 26
Béton Hurlant (skatepark), 33, 35
Biebel, Brandon, 96, 103

Big Brother, 62, 84
Big Four (voir Wallenberg), 105, 106
Big O (skatepark), 38, 39
Billabong, 78
Biniak, Bob, 21, 22, 23
Birdhouse, 60, 61, 62, 69, 71, 74, 77, 85, 98
Black Flag, 42, 50
Black Label, 55, 62, 74, 76, 81, 92, 105
Black, Frank, 82
Black, Noel, 17
Blackhart, Rick, 31, 33, 41
Blackout, 81
Blagnac (skatepark), 57
Blake, Tom, 11, 100
Blank, Squeak, 14
Bledsoe, Tyler, 103
Blender, Neil, 38, 40, 56
Blind, 52, 53, 58, 61, 62, 63, 68, 87, 91, 105
Block Shopping Mall (skatepark), 71
Blockhead, 57, 62
Blue, 61, 63
Blueprint, 91, 96
Blümen, Jürgen, 104
Blur, 76
Boglio, Al, 105
Bolster, Warren, 28
Bon appétit, 69
Bones Brigade, 34, 38, 39, 40, 41, 42, 43, 46, 47, 48, 49, 51, 53, 56, 61
Bones, 27, 52
Boost Mobile Pro Contest (Las Vegas, Nevada), 82
Bootleg, 96
Borden, Iain, 78
Bordertown (skatepark), 99
Boulala, Ali, 72, 79
Bourges (skate camp), 43, 45, 47, 57
Bourne, Scott, 85
Bowie, David, 82

Bowl, 24, 28, 29, 32, 33, 34, 36, 38, 39, 45, 55, 57, 75, 79, 83, 90
Bowman, Brad, 37
Boyce, Rob "Sluggo", 73
Boykin, Christopher, 99 "Big Black", 99
Boyle, Bod, 57, 105
Brady, Danny, 96
Brauch, Tim, 55, 62
Brenes, Chico, 103
Brentwood (Highschool), 21
Brezinski, Joey, 103
Brittain, Grant, 41, 43
Brixlegg, see Cradle Skatepark, 76
Brolin, Josh, 45
Brooke, Michael, 73
Brookings (skatepark), 76
Brophy, Andrew, 105
Brown, Bruce, 15
Brown, Don, 40, 44
Brown, Jake, 84, 94, 101
Brusk, 90
Bucchieri, Diego, 105
Bufoni, Leticia, 107
Built to Grind, 84
Built to Shred, 104
Bukowski, Charles, 18, 88
Bullard, Adrien, 106
Burgin, Oli, 68
Burnquist, Bob, 70, 72, 75, 84, 94, 96, 99, 102, 107
Burnside (skatepark), 56, 67, 76, 87, 99, 100
Burnside, Cara Beth, 70,
Busenitz, Dennis, 103, 106
Butte, Meyers, 11
Caballero, Steve, 15, 37, 38, 39, 41, 42, 43, 45, 46, 47, 51, 53, 54, 61, 72, 94
Cadillac Wheel, 20, 21, 22
Cahill, Chris, 22
California Games, 52
Calogirou, Claire, 74, 80

INDEX

Campbell, Kareem, 61, 62, 72
Campbell, Thomas, 70, 85
Cao, Jimmy, 103
Capaldi, Mike Mo, 96, 103, 104
Cardiel, John, 60, 62, 64, 81
Cardone, Daniel, 92, 94
Carey, Brainard, 76
Carlin, Jimmy, 106
Carlsbad (gap), 24, 26, 28, 63
Carlsbad (skatepark), 65
Carney, Jason, 56
Carnie, Dave, 85
Caron, Amy, 107
Carroll, Mike, 25, 57, 65, 67, 68, 72, 96, 97, 103
Carter, Chris, 56
Cash Money Vagrant, 82
Cassimus, James, 36
Castillo, Daniel, 103
Chalfant, Henry, 85
Chalmers, Alex, 92
Channel Street (skatepark), 99
Channita, Pat, 64
Chaos, 62
Charnoski, Rick, 107
Chasing Amy, 66
Cheever, révérend T., 10
Chehalem Skatepark (Newberg,Oregon), 74
Cherry Hill (skatepark), 32, 39
Chicago Roller Skate Company, 11, 13, 16
Chicago Trucks, 16
Childress, Chet, 78, 98
Chocolate, 63, 82
Chuck Taylor, 31, 105
Cincinnati Contemporary Art Center (Ohio)
Circa, 72
City of Quartz, 80
Clark, Larry, 66, 81, 82, 85
Clay wheels, 12, 13, 14, 16, 20

Cliché, 69, 78, 94, 96, 105
Cliver, Sean, 84, 85
Cockroach, 56, 52
Colinet, Jean-Pierre, 57
Coliseum, 79, 87
Color, 21, 61, 63, 85
Concrete Wave (skatepark), 28, 29, 73, 74
Confort moderne (Poitiers, France), 74
Conklin, Lance, 56
Connolly, Cynthia, 85
Consolidated, 61, 71, 74
Constantineau, Paul, 22, 23, 24
Converse, 105
Convic, 93
Cook, James, 9
Courtland, Vernon, 31
Coxon, Graham, 76
Cozens, Peggy, 40, 41
Cradle Skatepark (The), 76
Creager, Ronnie, 75, 87
Creative Urethane, 20, 21
Crimson, 92
Crocket, Gilbert, 106
Crowe, Cameron, 66
Cruise, Tom, 11, 66
Crum, Mike, 84, 85
Crum, Robert, 84, 85
Cruz, Penelope, 66
Cullen, Paul, 23
Da Deal is Dead, 62
Daclin, Jérémie, 69, 105
Dal Santo, Marissa, 105, 107
Danforth, Bill, 48
Danger Dave, 108
Danger, 49, 86, 108
Darkstar, 105
Davis, Garry Scott, 41, 80, 85
Davis, Mike, 41, 80, 85
Dawson, Cris, 22, 82
Dawson, Kimya, 22, 82
DC, 64, 72, 74, 81, 83, 86, 99
Death Box, 64
Death In Vegas, 82
Death, 64, 82

Debby does Blockhead, 62
Del Mar Nationals (contest), 23
Del Mar Skate Ranch (skatepark), 32, 33, 41, 44, 45
Deluxe, 55, 64, 97
Demain, Adrian, 42, 43
Demart, Fred, 95
Der Laufe der Ringe, 95
Descendents, 50
Design of Cities, 89
Destroy Everything Now, 78
Destructo, 68
Devo, 37
Dias, Sandro, 84, 94
Diaz, Cameron, 66
Dinosaur Jr, 56, 67, 107
Disposable, 84, 85
Dixon, Antwuan, 91
Documenta (Cassel, Allemagne), 80
Dog Bowl (pool), 29, 32
Dogtown – The Legend of the Z-Boys, 75, 77
Dogtown (Los Angeles, Californie), 19, 20, 21, 22, 24, 32, 33, 68, 73,
Dogtown and Z-Boys, 24
Dogtown Skateboard, 27, 31, 34, 47, 48, 65, 86
Dollin, Dustin, 91
Dominick, Ed, 78
Dompierre, Nick, 105, 106
Donnelly, Brian, 85
Dora, Miki, 12
Dorfman, Brad, 40, 42, 46, 49, 53, 55
Douglas, Steve, 62
Downhill Motion, 24, 26
Dreamland, 56, 76, 81
Dressen, Eric, 45, 54
Droors Clothing, 64
Duffel, Corey, 72, 106
Duffs, 64
Duffy, Pat, 58, 60, 61, 64, 69, 89
Dunlap, Kevin, 43, 66

143

Dunlap, Richie, **43, 66**
Dunn, Cheryl, **85**
Duperey, Anny, **34**
DVS, **66, 83, 103**
Dwindle distribution, **105**
Dyrdek, Rob, **27, 83, 99, 101, 103, 107**
<u>Dysfunctional</u>, **79, 74**
<u>Eastern Exposure 3: Underachievers</u>, **67**
Eastpak, **83**
Ecko, **78**
El Toro Highschool (Orange County, Californie), **94**
Element, **61, 78, 81**
<u>Elementality</u>, **81**
Elguera, Eddie, **34, 37, 38**
Ellington, Erik, **103**
Ellis, Jason, **84**
EMB (San Francisco, Californie), **45, 59, 65**
Embarcadero, voir EMB, **45, 59, 63, 65, 83**
Emerica, **66, 75**
<u>Endless Lines</u>, **80**
Endless Wave (skatepark), **32, 33**
Engblom, Skip, **13, 18, 20, 22, 42, 46, 49, 62, 87**
Enjoi, **74, 105**
Ermico, **31**
éS, **66, 74, 75, 77, 96, 102**
Escondido (réservoir), **24**
ESPN, **66**
Etnics, **53**
Etnies, **53, 64, 66, 74, 78**
Eurocana (skate camp), **39, 41, 43**
Europa, **69**
Eustache, Nicolas, **103**
Evans, Greg, **44, 96**
Evol Footwear, **64**
Evol, **62, 64**
Extreme Games, see X-Games, **66, 68, 70**
EZ Skateboards, **23**

Faction (The), **42, 47**
Fairey, Shepard, **85**
Fairfax, Benny, **103, 105**
Fallen, **81, 83, 103**
FDR Bridge, see Phillyside, **67**
<u>Feaster</u>, **62, 98**
Feil, Vivien, **103**
Fellers, Sierra, **106**
Fergusson, Tony, **63**
Fernandez, Cesar, **106**
Field, Matt, **56, 71, 92, 107**
Firehose, **50**
Fisher, Jerry, **67**
Fishli et Weiss
Fitzpatrick, Jim, **15, 68**
Flip, **39, 41, 64, 75, 77, 78, 82, 89, 92, 94, 97**
Folmer, Mike, **37**
Forbes, Israel, **62**
Forbes, Justin, **43**
Forbes, Reese, **67, 75**
Foundation, **53, 64, 83**
Four Star, **72**
Fowler, Ethan, **65, 72**
Fox, Michael J., **43, 44, 83**
Frac PACA (Marseille, France), **80**
Frazier, Mike, **60, 65, 66**
<u>Free Basin</u>, **75, 80, 85**
<u>Freedom Fries</u>, **69**
<u>Freedom of Choice</u>, **37, 61**
<u>Freestyler</u>, **34, 35, 40, 51, 53, 70, 74, 88, 99**
Freeth, George, **10, 11**
Friedberg, Josh, **62**
Friedman, Glen E., **29, 65, 68, 70, 75, 77, 85**
Fries, John, **14, 19, 69**
<u>From Deathbowl to Downtown</u>, **107**
Frost, Phil, **70, 85**
Frusciante, John, **82**
<u>Fuck you All</u>, **71**

<u>Fuck you Heroes</u>, **65, 68, 71**
<u>Fuck you Too</u>, **68, 71**
Fuel TV, **104**
<u>Fully Flared</u>, **96, 97, 98, 99, 107**
Fun Land (skatepark), **26**
Funkadelic, **82**
Furby, **103, 106**
Futura, **85**
<u>Future Primitive</u>, **43**
Gagnon, Pierre-Luc, **79, 82, 84, 101, 107**
Gallant, Ryan, **89**
Gallo, Pierre, **33**
Galloway, Benji, **94**
Game of skate, **102**
Gang Green, **42**
Garcia, Danny, **106**
Garcia, Gregory Thomas, **106**
Gatlyn, Josiah, **106**
Gavin, Tim, **63, 66**
Gelfand, Alan "Ollie", **14, 29, 30, 35, 36, 37, 38, 39**
Gerwer, Frank, **105**
Gesner, Eli, **62**
Getz, Kerry, **106**
Giant Distribution, **67, 62**
<u>Gidget</u>, **14, 12, 13**
Gillet, J.B., **96**
Gilley, Ben, **76**
Girard, Justin, **55, 64**
Girl, **68, 12, 15, 22, 63, 64, 65, 67, 68, 81, 82, 87, 88, 89, 96, 103, 104**
Gizmo Wheels, **53, 49**
Gladwell, Shaun, **99, 100**
Glifberg, Rune, **62, 64, 72, 77, 79, 99**
Globe, **64**
Glory Hole (full-pipe), **28**
Go for it, **30, 26**
Godard, Jean Luc, **17**
Goikoetxea, Alain, **94**
Golden State Wheel Company, **69**
<u>Goldfish</u>, **68, 63**
Goldwater, Barry, **28**

INDEX

Gonz Gap (San Francisco, Californie), **45, 59, 63**
Gonzales, David, **106**
Gonzales, Mark, **18, 38, 40, 42, 44, 45, 47, 50, 51, 52, 55, 58, 63, 68, 70, 85, 105**
Gordon & Smith, **23, 25, 38, 44, 92**
Gore, Ben, **106**
Grabke, Claus, **39, 44, 50, 51**
Graham, Dan, **55**
Graham, Jack, **24**
Grant Britain, J., **84**
Greathouse, Shiloh, **72**
Greco, Jim, **91**
Grimes, Marty, **23**
Groeneveld, Laurens, **101**
Groening, Matt, **55**
Groholski, Tom, **40**
Grosso, Jeff, **44, 76, 94**
Grundy, Guy, **24, 27**
Guerrero, Nicky, **44, 47**
Guerrero, Tommy, **18, 38, 40, 43, 44, 46, 51, 55, 85, 103**
Guiness Book, **101**
Gullwing, **25**
H-Street, **48, 49, 50, 53, 54, 55, 56, 57, 62, 96**
Habitat, **98, 103**
Hackett, Dave et Paul, **30**
Halprin, Lawrence, **45**
Hamm, Keith, **98**
Hammer Head, , **92**
Happy Mondays, **82**
Hardwicke, Catherine, **86**
Haring, Keith, **85**
Harithi, Sami, **62**
Harley Davidson, **18**
Harris, Kevin, **38, 43, 46, 51**
Hart, Kelly, **106**
Haslam, Chris, **37, 106**
Hassan, Omar, **59, 76, 77, 81, 94**
Hastings, Todd, **42**
Hawaiian Surfboard, **11**

Hawk, Occupation: Skateboarder, **77**
Hawk, Tony, **18, 38, 41, 42, 43, 44, 45, 46, 47, 51, 54, 55, 57, 59, 60, 63, 64, 66, 69, 70, 71, 72, 73, 77, 84, 96**
Hawkins, Lyn-Z Adams, **96**
He'e nalu, **10, 11**
Hecox, Evan, **85**
Hedges, Jeff, **51**
Hello Jojo, **69**
Hendrix, Neil, **76, 84**
Hensley, Matt, **51, 54, 57, 61, 76**
Herman, Bryan, **45, 103**
Hester Series (contest), **33, 34**
Heuty, Jean-François, **29**
Hewitt, Peter, **81**
Hill, Frankie, **20, 50, 56, 60**
Hill, Mike, **56, 98**
Hilton, Barron, **14, 18**
Hilton, Dave et Steve, **14, 18**
Hirata, Frank, **56**
Ho, Jeff, **18, 22, 23**
Hobie, **13, 14, 15, 16, 23**
Hocking, Justin, **85**
Hoffart, Jordan, **106**
Holknet, Per, **41**
Holt, Nancy, **28**
Hopps, **92**
Hosoï Skateboards, **40, 46, 92**
Hosoï, Christian, **37, 38, 40, 41, 43, 45, 46, 47, 50, 51, 54, 92, 98**
Howard, Rick, **57, 63, 67, 72, 96, 97, 106**
Howell, Andy, **55, 60, 61, 62, 64,**
Howell, Ocean, **60, 77, 78**
Howell, Russ, **24**
Hubba Hideout (ledge), **59**
Hubbard, Mark, **56, 76**
Humco, **12**

Humpston, Wes, **22, 43**
Hunt, Greg, **107**
Huston, Nyjah, **96, 101, 106**
Hyde Park Arts Center (Chicago), **75**
Ibaseta, Rick, **44**
Independent, **31, 32, 37, 41, 55, 62, 67, 68, 84**
Inhabitant, **98, 103**
Inland Surf Shop (The), **30**
Insane Terrain, **77**
International Association of Skateboard Companies, **68**
Interpol, **82**
INXS, **44**
IPath, **71**
Iverson, Chris, **42, 43**
Jackson, Jo, **82, 85**
Jackson, Michael, **82, 85**
Jan and Dean, **15**
Janoski, Stefan, **106**
Jart, **91**
Jarvis, James, **85**
Jefferson, Atiba, **84**
Jenkins, Andy, **85**
Jensen, Nick, **96**
Jepsen, Hal, **22, 26, 37**
Jesse, Jason, **47, 61, 105**
JFA, **46, 42**
JFK Plazza, see Love Park
Johanson, Chris, **85**
Johnson, Marc, **74, 87, 96, 98, 103**
Johnson, Rudy, **53, 58**
Johnson, Torger, **18, 23**
Jonze, Spike, **56, 58, 63, 67, 82, 85, 96**
Joy Division, **82**
Juice, **14, 63**
Justin Herman Plazza, see EMB
Jutra, Claude, **17**
Kalis, Josh, **106**
Kasaï, Lester, **38, 45**
Kaupas, Natas, **19, 38, 40, 42, 45, 50, 51, 53, 56, 57**
Kelso (skatepark), **17**
Ken Park, **81**

Kendall, Jeff, **50**
Kennedy, Cory, **106**
Kenter Canyon Elementary School (Los Angeles, Californie), **21**
Kerouac, Jack, **18**
Kettering Skate Plaza (skatepark), **83, 90**
Kicktail, **19, 31**
Kids, **66, 81**
Kilgallen, Margaret, **85**
King, James, **9**
King, Jeff, **104**
Kingpin, **22, 35, 79, 87, 88, 109**
Kirchart, Heat, **56, 65, 69, 71, 106**
Klein, Jeremy, **53, 60, 71**
Klindt, Jeff, **55**
Knievel, Evel, **36, 79**
Knigge, Ron, **55**
Knox, Tom, **54, 56**
Knutson, Jeff, **85**
Kohner, Frederik, **12**
Kohner, Kathy "Gidget", **12**
Kona (skatepark), **32, 99**
Kona Bowl (pool), **32**
Kop, Johnee, **45**
Korine, Harmony, **66, 73, 81, 85**
Koston, Eric, **25, 57, 63, 67, 68, 72, 75, 82, 96, 97, 102, 103**
Král, Zach, **101**
Krosigk, Holger von, **104**
Krux Kickflips Challenges, **101**
Kryptonics, **22**
Kubo, Shogo, **22, 26**
La Bassine (skatepark), **99**
La Beauté, **75**
La Caverne (skatepark), **99**
La Croisière du Snark, **10**
Label Kills, **76**
Lachman, Ed, **81**
Ladd, P. J., **79, 82, 87, 89, 103**
Lafayette Park (skatepark), **107**
Lakai, **72, 83, 96, 97, 98, 107**

Lakewood (skatepark), **38, 39**
Lamar, Bert, **37**
Landscape, **46, 56**
Lasek, Bucky, **49, 72, 73, 82, 101**
Lavigne, Avril, **81**
La Villette (skatepark), **33, 35, 100**
Layton, Jhonny, **103**
Le Grand-Bornand (contest), **57, 59**
Le Skate, un jeu, **74**
Le Tigre, **82**
Leap of Faith (gap), **69**
Lee Jeans, **83**
Lee, Jason, **20, 51, 53, 56, 58, 61, 62, 64, 66**
Lefebvre, Henri, **78**
Leuret, Gabriel, **62**
Lewis, Jeffrey, **82**
Lick, **62**
Life, **57, 61**
Life & Limb, **85**
Life Magazine, **12, 16**
Lincoln City (skatepark), **81**
Logan Earth Ski, **23, 27**
Logan, Brad, **18**
Logan, Bruce, **18**
Londinsky, Michel, **33**
London, Jack, **10, 70**
Long, Kevin "Spanky", **91**
Longwood (skatepark), **29**
Lopes, Joe, **44**
Lorient (skatepark), **33**
Losi, Allen, **27, 39**
Losi, Raymond H., **27, 39**
Louis Vuitton, **105**
Love Child, **62**
Love Park (Philadelphie), **65, 83, 89, 90**
Lucero Skateboard, **46**
Lucero, John, **38, 39, 44, 46, 55, 62**
Lutzka, Greg, **82, 102, 106**
Mac Fetridge, Geoff, **85**
Mac Gee, Barry, **85**

Mac Gyver, **104**
Macba (Barcelone, Espagne), **90**
Macdonald, Andy, **68, 70, 79, 84**
Made For Skate, **104**
Madrid, **44, 92**
Magnusson, Tony, **44, 48, 50, 57, 62, 64, 94**
Maher, Jared Jacang, **85**
Makaha Skateboard, **12, 14, 15, 16, 18, 19, 23, 25**
Maldonado, Mike, **67**
Mallrats, **66**
Maloof Money Cup (contest), **99, 101, 106**
Malto, Sean, **103, 104**
Manfre, Tony, **105**
Marcopoulos, Ari, **85**
Marginal Way (skatepark, Seattle), **99**
Mariano, Guy, **53, 58, 63, 96, 97, 98, 99, 106, 107**
Marina Del Rey (skatepark), **32, 37, 38**
Markovich, Kris, **57, 60, 63, 78, 92**
Marks, Billy, **96, 103, 104**
Martelleur, David, **108**
Martinez, Jessie, **46**
Mascis, Jay, **107**
Mayhew, Dave, **68**
McClouth, Nick, **103**
McCrank, Rick, **72, 75**
McEntire, Cody, **106**
McEntire, Mike, **50, 108**
McFly, Marty, **43, 44**
McGill, Mike, **14, 35, 37, 39, 41, 42, 43, 46, 61**
McGinley, Ryan, **85**
McGinness, Ryan, **85**
McKay, Colin, **49, 57, 58, 61, 64, 66, 70, 89**
McKee, Marc, **52, 68**
McNatt, Adam, **57**
McRad, **42**

Melcher, Patrick, 72
Memory Screen, 62, 107
Mendizabal, Javier, 69
Menezes, Rodrigo, 66
Menikmati, 75, 77
Metallica, 46, 42
Middlesbrough (skate plazza), 90
Mike Vallely Animal Farm, 54, 49
Miller, Chris, 38, 47, 48, 55, 57, 71, 94
Mills, Mike, 70, 85
Milton Keynes (skate plazza), 90
Mind Field, 107
Mob, 91
Montaño, Cesario, 98
Montoya, Danny, 103
Moore, Aly, 44
Morrow, Bill, 94
Mortagne, Fred, 75, 78
Mortimer, Sean, 77, 84
Mosley, Gershon, 68
Mount Baldy, 19, 21, 24, 28, 100
Mountain, Lance, 38, 40, 42, 43, 46, 47, 54, 60, 68, 91, 92, 94
Mouse, 67, 82, 96
Muir, Jim, 22, 27, 47, 87
Muir, Mike, 47
Mullen, Rodney, 18, 30, 34, 35, 37, 38, 39, 40, 41, 42, 43, 46, 49, 51, 53, 54, 58, 64, 68, 72, 74, 84, 87, 96, 105
Mullus, Pat "Muckus", 19
Münster (contest), 39, 45, 47, 51, 54, 57, 59, 62, 63, 65, 66, 68, 70, 72, 73, 75, 77, 79, 82, 84, 94, 99
Muska, Chad, 56, 72
Musso, Bruno, 44
My Name is Earl, 91
Nas, 82
Nasworthy, Frank, 20, 22
Neeson, Niall, 85

Nelson, Blake, 100
Nesser, Steve, 105
New Deal, 55, 57, 58, 61, 62, 64
New Pipeline, (skatepark), 81
New York Times, 77, 100
Next Generation, 62
Ngoho, Pat, 94
Nguyen, Don, 94
NHS, 20, 22, 31, 34, 37, 40, 46, 49, 50
Nichols, Coan, 107
Nike SB, see Nike, 78, 98, 107
Nike, 71, 78, 83, 98, 107
Nolder, Monty, 39
Nothing But The Truth, 98, 107
Novak, Richard, 20
Noway, 54, 57, 80
Nunn, Ken, 73
O'Connor, Tim, 67
O'Malley, John, 24
Oakmont Drive Ramp (quarter-pipe), 29
Oasis (skatepark), 37
Oceanside (contest), 35, 45, 46
Octopus, 104
Oki, Peggy, 22, 23
Olson, Alex, 96, 103, 104, 107
Olson Brothers, 9
Olson, Steve, 31, 33, 34, Orange County Museum of Art (Californie), 85
Orsi, Agi, 73
Ortiz, Chris, 62
Osiris, 64
Oyola, Ricky, 67, 92
P. J. Ladd's Wonderful Horrible Life, 87
P.O.P., see The Cove, 18
Pacific Ocean Pier, see The Cove, 18
Paez, Jesse, 105
Page, Ty, 18, 23, 72, 84, 86, 87
Palais de Tokyo (Paris), 80
Pang, Jeff, 44
Pappas, Tas, 73

Paraponaris, Hervé, 80
Paris (skatepark), 28
Pastras, Chris "Dune", 44, 61, 63
Paul Revere Junior High School, 19, 21
Paved Wave (skatepark), 26
Pavement, 65, 67
Payne, Tim, 46, 51, 52, 69, 71
Pena Jr, Julian, 37
Penn, Sean, 77
Penny, Tom, 64, 75, 79
Peralta, Stacy, 12, 21, 22, 23, 25, 26, 27, 31, 34, 35, 36, 37, 39, 40, 41, 42, 45, 46, 58, 73, 77, 82, 87
Perelson, Alex, 107
Peters, Duane, 31, 33, 36, 37, 38, 54, 69, 76, 94, 98
Peterson, Clint, 103
Peterson, Leigh, 57
Petibled, 10
Pettibon, Raymond, 85
Pfanner, Chris, 105
Phelps, Jake, 103
Philippe Petit, 108
Philips, Jeff, 41
Phillips, Jim, 43
Phillips, Jimbo, 43
Phillyside (skatepark), 67
Pier 7 (San Francisco, Etats-Unis), 90, 106
Pier Avenue Junior High School (Los Angeles, Californie), 14
Pier Park (skatepark), 99
Pilote, 80
Pipeline (skatepark), 28, 29, 38, 51, 71
Plan B, 57, 58, 61, 63, 64, 68, 89
Planet Earth, 55
Plimpton, James, 10
Plum, Mike "Lizard King", 106
Port Orford (skatepark), 76
Pott, Andrew, 106
Powell Corporation, 27, 31

147

Powell Peralta, **31, 37, 38, 40, 41, 42, 43, 44, 46, 48, 49, 52, 54, 55, 56, 57, 58, 67, 71, 85, 91**
Powell, **58, 60, 61, 62, 92**
Powell, George, **21, 25, 27, 31, 58**
Powers, Steve, **85**
Prado (skatepark), **57**
Pratt, Nathan, **22, 30**
Pray For Me, **98**
Prime Time, **46**
Project 8, **96**
Propaganda, **56, 60, 67**
Protec Pool Party (contest), **94**
PS Stick, **53**
Psycho Stix (Vision), **44**
Public Domain, **49, 54**
Public Enemy, **82**
Pudwill, Torey, **105, 106**
Puig, Lucas, **69, 96, 97, 105, 106**
Puimarta, Tim, **34, 53**
Pulaski Park (Washington), **65**
Pushead, **85**
Quarterly Skateboarder, **15, 16, 23**
Questionable, **61**
Queyrel, Claude, **80**
Quicksilver Inc., **83**
Quicktail, **27**
Quicksilver, **25, 83, 86, 94**
Radials, **25**
Ragdoll, **72**
Raibal, Ruben, **68**
Ramondetta, Peter, **106**
Ramones, **63**
Rapp, Paul, **26**
Rasa Libre, **92**
Rat Bones, **37**
Real, **25, 55, 63, 103, 105**
Really Sorry, **82**
Reategui, Eddie, **42**
Rector, Mike, **27**
Red Hot Chili Peppers, **42, 52**

Reyes, Mic-E, **51**
Reynolds, Andrew, **34, 71, 72, 74, 94, 101, 103, 105, 106**
Richards, Bill, **13**
Richardson, Terry, **85**
Richter, Jordan, **53**
Ride On Skatepark (Newark, Californie), **33**
Ride The Sky, **103**
Ridgeway, Bryan, **40**
Riding The South Surf, **10**
Rieder, Dylan, **104, 107**
Right To Skate, **62**
Rincon Middle School (San Diego, Californie), **106**
Rip City, **42**
Rising Son, The Legend of Skateboarder Christian Hosoï, **98**
Road Rider, **22**
Rob and Black, **99**
Roberts, Chris, **103**
Robertson, Lindsey, **105**
Rocco, Steve, **34, 37, 38, 46, 49, 52, 53, 55, 57, 58, 62, 63, 64, 68, 72, 98**
Rodriguez, Gabriel, **57**
Rodriguez, Paul, **42, 78, 83, 89, 96, 101, 102, 106**
Rodriguez, Ray "Bones", **31, 35**
Rogers, Jeremy, **89**
Rogerson, David, **98**
Rogowski, Mark "Gator", **38, 44, 47, 55, 98**
Rojas, Clare E., **85**
Roll' Surf, **17**
Roller Derby, **12**
Roller Sports, **20, 21**
Rollerblade Inc., **9**
Rooler Gab (skatepark), **62**
Rose, Aaron, **70, 74, 85**
Roskopp, Rob, **50**
Rote Flora (skatepark), **99**
Rotten, Johnny, **79**
Roule ma ville, **80**

Rouli-Roulant, **17**
Round 3, **87**
Rousseau, J.-J., **69**
Rowley, Geoff, **27, 64, 72, 75, 79, 106**
Rubbish Heap, **53, 54**
Ruff, Billy, **38**
Ruml, Wentzle, **22, 23, 30**
Ryan, Tommy, **18, 55, 85, 89, 94, 96, 99, 101, 102**
S.O.M.
Saari, Arto, **72, 75, 77, 79, 92, 103**
Safe Spot, Skate Spot (see Lafayette Park), **107**
Saint-Jean-de-Luz (skatepark), **29**
Salabanzi, Bastien, **77, 79, 84, 92, 99**
Salazar, Omar, **98, 103, 104, 107**
Sanderson, Eric, **43**
Sandoval, Tommy, **105, 106**
Santa Cruz Surf Shop, **20**
Santa Cruz, **27, 31, 34, 37, 40, 41, 44, 46, 47, 49, 50, 51, 52, 53, 54, 55, 56, 57, 61, 62, 92, 107**
Santa Monica Airlines, **40, 42, 49** see also SMA
Santa Monica, see also Dogtown (Californie), **10, 13, 18, 19, 29, 32, 38, 42**
Santiago, Coco, **44**
Santos, Willy, **60, 70, 72, 98**
Sarlo, Alan, **22**
Savannah Side (skatepark), **79, 83**
Scarface, **82**
Schatz, Adam, **62**
Schilleref, Johnny, **64**
Schmid, Daniel, **104**
Schmitt Stix, **35, 39, 42, 43, 44, 46, 48, 55, 89**

INDEX

Schmitt, Paul, **35, 39, 42, 44, 53, 55, 62, 89**
Schock, Michael, **34**
Scooter skate, **44**
Scott, Mark, **41, 56, 76, 85**
Scroggs, Tim, **35**
Second Hand Smoke, **64**
Segovia, Patty, **70**
Senatore, Kent, **37, 69**
Sénizergues, Pierre-André, **44, 53, 66, 74, 104**
Senn, Chris, **66, 72, 94**
Shackle me not, **50, 54**
Shannon, Shuriken, **105**
Sheckler, Ryan, **55, 94, 96, 101, 102**
Sheffey, Sean, **44, 57, 63**
Sherwood, Kent, **20, 23**
Shier, Paul, **103**
Shreveport (skate plaza), **93**
Shuirman, Jay, **20**
Shut, **35, 44, 61**
Sick Boys, **51, 108**
Sidewalk surfboard, **12**
Silver, Tony, **13, 85**
SIMPARCH, **75, 80, 85**
Simpson, Bart, **55**
Sims, **22, 25, 31, 34, 35, 37, 38, 40, 42, 44, 46, 49, 53**
Skate and Destroy, **41, 42, 47**
Skate City, (skatepark), **40**
Skate France International, **30, 34**
Skate France Magazine, **30**
Skate Gang, **45**
Skate Hi, **27**
Skate in the Shade (skatepark), **32**
Skate Magazine, **34, 57, 62, 65**
Skate More, **91, 95**
Skate or Die, **52**
Skate Plaza Foundation, **83**
Skate Story, **74**
Skateboard (magazine), **30, 34**

Skateboard Madness, **37**
Skateboard Museum (Stuttgart, Allemagne), **104**
Skateboarder, **23, 26, 27, 28, 30, 31, 34, 36, 37, 70, 75**
"Skateboarding is not a crime"
Skateboarding, Space and the City, **78**
Skater Dater, **17**
Skater of the year (Skateboarder), **34**
Skater of the year (Thrasher), **62, 63, 65, 68, 70, 73, 79, 84, 94, 99, 103**
SkaterCross (skatepark), **28**
Skatin', **34**
Skatopia (skatepark), **33**
Skee Skate, **14**
Skidmore, Owings, **45**
Skull Skate, **42**
Slalom, **23, 24, 47**
Slam City Jam (contest), **68**
Slap, **62, 104**
SMA (see also Santa Monica Airlines), **42, 46, 49, 55, 57, 61**
SMA Rocco Division, **46, 49**
Smith, Dan, **37**
Smith, Jay, **37**
Smith, Kevin, **66**
Smith, Rodney, **62**
SMP Skatepark, (Shanghai, Chine), **93**
Smythe, John (see also Craig Stecyk), **23**
Social Distortion, **42**
Sole Technologie, **74**
Solid Surf (skatepark), **28, 29**
Solomine, John, **31**
Soma, **106**
Song, Daewon, **25, 68, 87, 91, 94, 95, 96, 103**
Sonic Youth, **50, 56**
Sorry, **78, 82**

South Bank (Londres, Angleterre), **28**
Speed Freaks, **56, 107**
Speedwheels, **49, 52**
Spencer, Terry, **14**
Speyer, Wade, **59, 60, 65, 76, 77**
Spin Magazine, **73, 87**
Spitfire, **55**
Sprouse, Stephen, **105**
Staab, Kevin, **42, 43, 45, 47**
Stanton, Darrell, **89, 101, 105**
Stapelbäddsparken (skatepark), **94**
Steadham, Steve, **42, 43**
Steamer, Elissa, **67, 70, 73, 107**
Stecyk, Craig R., **18, 23, 26, 27, 30, 37, 41, 43, 65, 74, 75, 77, 85**
Steppe Side (skatepark), **83**
Stereo, **63, 65, 103, 105**
Stevenson, Larry, **13, 14, 19**
Stickler, Helen, **98**
Stoked: The Rise and Fall of Gator, **98**
Storm Sequence, **99**
Strain, Donovan, **103**
Stranger, Julian, **51, 64**
Streets on Fire, **51, 54, 60**
Strike, Christian, **85**
Sturt, Dan, **70**
Style 38, (voir Skate Hi), **27**
Sugar, **70**
Suicidal Tendencies, **42, 47**
Sun Tunnels, **28**
Sundance Film Festival, **77**
Supa, Danny, **103**
Super Session, **22, 26**
Super Skateboard, **34**
Superchunk, **67**
Surf De Earth (skatepark), **32**
Surf Guide, **13**
Svitak, Kristian, **76, 92**

Swank, Tod, **53, 64**
Swanson, Gary, **14**
Swastika Surfboard Company, **11**
Sweet, David, **12, 15, 82**
Swenson, Eric, **31**
Swift, Dave, **72, 84**
Syndrome Distribution, **89**
Takakjian, Andy, **44**
Talking Heads, **37**
Tanner, Steve, **14**
Taylor, Grant, **104, 107**
Taylor, Mikey, **103**
Templeton, Ed, **20, 51, 55, 57, 61, 63, 64, 65, 66, 67, 80, 85**
Tensor, **74, 105**
Ternasky, Mike, **48, 50, 57, 58, 63, 64**
Texeira, Rodrigo, **75**
Thatcher, frères, **28**
The Acme Skateboard Video, **62**
The Answer is Never, **79, 80, 85, 107**
The Berrics (skatepark), **102, 103, 106**
The Bones Brigade Video Show, **41, 42, 43**
The Concrete Wave, **73, 74**
The Cove, **18, 19**
The DC Video, **81, 99**
The Devil's Toy, **81**
The End, **71**
The Endless Summer, **15**
The Essential Disturbance, **80**
The Firm, **61, 62**
The Forks (skatepark), **93**
The Golden Age of Neglect, **80**
The Life of Ryan, **99**
The Lords of Dogtown, **86**
The Man Who Souled The World, **98**
The Mutt, **84**
The North Face, **83**
The Poetics of Security, **77**

The Ranch (skatepark), **38**
The Search for Animal Chin, **46**
The Shred Sled Symposium, **70**
The Skateboard Mag, **84, 98, 99**
The Strongest of the Strange, **88, 109**
Thiebaud, Jim, **50, 51, 55**
This is not the New H-Street Video, **56**
Thomas, Chet, **50, 56, 68,**
Thomas, Jamie, **27, 56, 66, 67, 69, 72, 73, 76, 81, 90, 91, 103, 106**
Thrasher, **37, 38, 40, 41, 54, 57, 59, 62, 63, 68, 70, 72, 73, 77, 82, 84, 86, 88, 90, 94, 99, 103, 105**
Thrashin', **45**
Thread Waxing Space (New York), **70**
Thrill of it All, **69**
Thunder, **55, 68**
Tim and Henry's Pack of Lies, **62**
Tim Tim, Chad, **103**
Time Magazine, **48**
Tintin, **17, 80**
Titus Skate, **39**
Todd, James, **42, 85**
Toft, Lonnie, **25, 31**
Tony Hawk Pro Skater, **72, 73**
Torres, Vanessa, **84**
Touche, Marc, **74, 80**
Toxic, **52**
Toy Machine, **63, 64, 65, 66, 67, 76, 103, 104**
Tracker, **22, 40, 41**
Tracy, Terry "Tubesteak", **12**
Traffic, **92**
Transworld, **41, 43, 53, 70, 72, 74, 83, 84, 86, 90, 94, 99, 100**

Trapasso, Nick, **104, 106**
Trauma
Tricks, **70**
Trocadéro bleu citron, **34**
Troy, Chris, **105**
Truck, **11, 21, 22, 25, 26, 32, 34, 35, 41, 59, 60, 74, 84, 97, 98**
Truffaut, François, **17**
Trujillo, Tony, **39, 72, 79, 81, 82, 84**
Tum Yeto, **64, 66**
Tura, David, **95**
Turner, Jovantae, **63**
Turning Point Ramp, **36, 37**
TV, **61, 99, 104**
Tyers, Robert John, **10**
Tylenol, **84**
Ueda, Lincoln, **92**
Uncle Wiggly's, **44**
Underhill, Ray, **43**
Underworld Element, **61**
Union, **61, 62**
United Skate Front, **40**
Upland, **28, 38, 79, 81, 94**
Ursulines (Bruxelles, Belgique), **90**
Vaissette, Jean-Marc, **47**
Val Surf (Los Angeles, Californie), **13**
Valdez, Bobby, **31, 39, 41**
Vallely, Mike, **20, 45, 49, 50, 52, 56, 58, 61, 63, 76, 77, 96, 106, 107**
Van Doren Rubber Company, **16**
Van Doren, frères, **16, 25**
Van Sant, Gus, **100**
Vancouver (skate plazza), **51, 68, 90**
Vandals (The), **42**
Vanilla Sky, **66**
Vans, **16, 25, 27, 53, 61, 64, 71, 78, 83**
Variflex, **38**
Velzy, **13**

Ventura, Sergie, 92
Venture, 68
VF Corporation, 83
Video Days, 58, 61, 105
Virtual Reality, 63
Vision Street Wear, 40, 53
Vision, 31, 35, 40, 42, 44, 46, 49, 52, 53, 55, 61
Vitello, Fausto, 31, 37, 41, 55
Vogel, Dirk, 104
Volito, 10
Walker Skateboard, 35
Wallenberg (gap), 58, 105
Wallos (ditch), 24, 25, 26, 47
Warhol, Andy, 85
Washington Street (skatepark), 99
Wassup Rockers, 95
Waterman, Jack, 42
Watson, Dan, 97
Way, Damon, 64
Way, Danny, 21, 48, 49, 53, 54, 56, 57, 58, 59, 60, 61, 64, 70, 73, 79, 81, 84, 86, 89, 94, 99, 102
Weaver, Greg, 24
Webster, John, 40
Welcome to Hell, 66, 67, 76
Welinder, Per, 41, 42, 43, 44, 46, 60, 71
Wenning, Brian, 89
West Linn (skatepark), 81
Westgate, Brandon, 105
Weyland, Jocko, 79, 80, 85, 107
Whaley, Ron, 62
What if?, 97, 91
Wheels of Fire, 50, 54
White, Shaun, 27, 101
Who Cares? The Duane Peters Story, 27
Williams, Jahmal, 67, 92, 96
Williams, Stevie, 67, 92, 96
Wills, Spyder, 24

Wilson, Jeron, 103
Winchester (skatepark), 32
Winkel, Willi, 25
Wolfe, Dan, 67
Woman's Home Companion, 10
Woodward, Woody, 14
World industries, 49, 52, 53, 54, 57, 58, 59, 60, 61, 62, 63, 68, 72, 85
Wrangler, 83
Wray, Jeremy, 60, 64, 65, 106
X-Games (contest), 70, 73, 74, 77, 84, 94, 99, 101
Yama, 91
Yang, Romon, 85
Yeah Right!, 82, 87, 88, 96
Yelland, Tobin, 85
Yerba Buena Art Center (San Francisco), 85
Yogoo Valley (skatepark), 26
Yohn, George, 44
Z-Boys, 22, 23, 24, 26, 29, 34, 73, 75, 77
Z-Flex, 23
Zattoni, Giogio, 73
Zemeckis, Robert, 43
Zephyr Shop, 18, 20
Zephyr Team, (see Z-Boys)
Zero, 55, 66, 69, 76, 81, 90, 105
ZMovie, 98
Zoo York, 62, 78, 105
Zorlac, 42

Supported by
carhartt.

Printed by CPI Firmin Didot (103456), France, in January 2011.